A Toolkit for Creative Teaching in Post-Compulsory Education

A Toolkit for Creative Teaching in Post-Compulsory Education

Linda Eastwood, Jennie Coates, Liz Dixon, Josie Harvey, Chris Ormondroyd and Sarah Williamson

Open University Press

Open University Press
McGraw-Hill Education
McGraw-Hill House
Shoppenhangers Road
Maidenhead
Berkshire
England
SL6 2QL

email: enquiries@openup.co.uk
world wide web: www.openup.co.uk

and Two Penn Plaza, New York, NY 10121–2289, USA

First published 2009

A catalogue record of this book is available from the British Library

ISBN–13: 9780335234165 (pb)   9780335234158 (hb)
ISBN–10: 033523416X (pb)   0335234151 (hb)

Library of Congress Cataloguing-in-Publication Data
CIP data applied for

Typeset by YHT Ltd, London
Printed in the UK by Bell and Bain Ltd, Glasgow

Fictitious names of companies, products, people, characters and/or data that may be used herein (in case studies or in examples) are not intended to represent any real individual, company, product or event.

Mixed Sources
Product group from well-managed
forests and other controlled sources
www.fsc.org   Cert no. TT-COC-002769
© 1996 Forest Stewardship Council
FSC

The *McGraw·Hill* Companies

Contents

List of Contributors

Jennie Coates is an experienced teacher, having taught vocational skills in both compulsory/post-compulsory and community education. She worked as an Advanced Skills teacher in FE for several years and has been involved in teacher education, both FE and HE, for the past 15 years.

Liz Dixon is a Senior Lecturer at the University of Huddersfield in the School of Education and Professional Development. Having trained originally as a nurse, Liz started working in further education, teaching on a range of vocational programmes before moving into post-compulsory teacher training. She now works at the university as a Teacher Trainer and has considerable experience of Pre-service and In-service PCET programmes. Her main research interests are in creativity, work-based learning and the academic lives of teacher trainers.

Linda Eastwood is a Principal Lecturer and Head of Division in the School of Education and Professional Development at the University of Huddersfield. She qualified originally as a primary school teacher, teaching in that area before moving into Further Education and Higher Education. Linda has worked at the university for 10 years and has taught on several programmes – but now specializes on the pre-service PGCE (PCET) course, having personal tutor responsibility for one of the social science groups. Her research interests are predominately in the area of creativity and innovation in the post-compulsory sector.

Josie Harvey is the TQEF leader for the 'Creativity and Innovation in Teaching in Higher Education' project and is also a Senior Lecturer in the School of Education and Professional Development at the University of Huddersfield. She originally trained as an accountant before working in Further Education and Higher Education where she has acquired 25 years of experience across all levels, teaching 14-year-olds to adults – specializing in finance. She also has 15 years experience as a Senior Curriculum Manager in Business in a large Further Education college, gaining extensive experience in staff development, curriculum design and operations. Currently she teaches on the pre-service PGCE (PCET) programme at the university and as part of the TQEF project runs Creativity Workshops – and has recently produced a DVD entitled *Creativity in Teaching*.

Chris Ormondroyd is a Senior Lecturer in Education in PCET in the School of Education and Professional Development at the University of Huddersfield. He has worked in the education sector for over 30 years, initially in Further Education and later in Higher Education. Chris has personal tutor responsibility for one of the PGCE/Cert Ed (PCET) social science groups. His research interests include theorization related to the sociology of knowledge recently linked to creativity and innovation.

Sarah Williamson is a Senior Lecturer in the School of Education and Professional Development at the University of Huddersfield. Her background was in art and design and design management before moving into teaching in the post-compulsory sector. She has worked as a Teacher Trainer for over 12 years in Further Education and Higher Education and currently teaches on the pre-service PGCE (PCET) programme at the university.

Acknowledgements

To all staff in the School of Education and Professional Development and to the students on the PGCE Cert Ed (PCET) course at the University of Huddersfield who have allowed us, tolerated us, worked with us to develop, try out, enhance and practise methods of creative teaching and learning and who have progressed and further developed the ideas we have suggested in their own teaching careers – their enthusiasm has been truly inspirational!

Introduction

You know how it is. You are with a group of people you haven't met before. You usually introduce yourself and then often the conversation moves into an exchange about what you all do for a living. Imagine such a conversation involving one of the authors of this book:

Q: ... and what exactly is it that you do?
A: I'm a Teacher Trainer. I train people who want to teach.
Q: In schools?
A: No, in the post-compulsory sector, 'PCET' for short.
Q: Oh, what's that, then? I don't think I've heard of PCET.

And therein lies something of the challenge and at the same time the excitement of teaching in PCET.

The post-compulsory education and training (PCET) sector encompasses a rich and diverse mix of teachers, trainers and learners. The learners include young people and adults; increasingly it also includes learners who are being offered teaching and learning which combines a school, a college and a selected workplace experience. Some learners attend courses because they want to and others because they are required to be there. The subject areas are equally diverse and varied including traditional academic and vocational disciplines, training and professional qualifications and recreational subjects. The courses and qualifications span all levels from pre-entry to degree level and everything in between.

Like other areas of education, the PCET sector, in response to social, political and economic trends, finds itself subject to fluctuation and change. It is required to be proactive in its response to interventions and initiatives and at the same time provide a valuable and worthwhile educational experience. As a consequence, those who teach in the sector need to be able to work within a highly challenging and often demanding environment. Teachers need to be able to teach varied groups and individual learners with a range of needs and requirements. From the start of their initial teaching practice and then throughout their careers, PCET teachers are likely to teach subjects they themselves are passionate and knowledgeable about, but also aspects of the curriculum about which they may have less passion or confidence. The same could be said about the learner: sometimes they will be intrigued and motivated, relishing the challenge of new or difficult learning, at other times they may find the going tough for all sorts of reasons and appear unreceptive and disinterested. The PCET practitioner may find themselves working in state-of-the-art colleges or much more modest sites with limited staffing and resources to draw upon.

Teachers need to be able to be flexible in becoming professional chameleons who can change their approach to suit a whole range of different circumstances. Some aspects of teaching will lend themselves well to didactic approaches where the teacher takes the lead and imparts knowledge and information. other times, learning is more likely to take place where a teacher assumes a facilitative position and it is here that the learner who takes the lead and assumes a more active role, while the teacher guides the learning to a greater or lesser extent. The decision as to the approach taken sits with the teacher and is part of their professional judgement. In any lesson, there is likely to be a degree of ebb and flow and vacillation, which an effective teacher will respond to. The chosen approach may be planned or intuitive depending on the situation at the time. Decisions will be made in the light of many factors including: the learners themselves, the subject being taught, the environment and resources available, the expertise and confidence of the teacher, to name but a few.

This book is intended to be a practical teaching and learning guide through ideas about how teachers in either schools, colleges, training organizations, universities or other PCET institutions might develop their own creative and innovative approaches to both creative teaching and creative learning. It is a book written *by* practitioners, *for* practitioners. The School of Education and Professional Development at the University of Huddersfield is a Centre for Excellence in PCET Teacher Training and this book will explore many of the creative and innovative approaches that have been used to enhance and develop our teacher training programmes. Creativity means different things to different people.

Ted Wragg (2003) writing in *The Guardian* argued:

> It is a pity that the notion of creativity in education has to be fought for or reclaimed, as it should be a central feature of teaching and learning. It is the crucial element in each generation's renewal and enhancement of itself. Without it, society would not even stand still. It would gradually roll backwards ... thinking up fresh ideas is what teachers are paid for.

When pre-service trainee teachers at Huddersfield University are introduced to the concept of creativity during their initial training, their definitions and responses while undertaking their teaching practice are varied and perhaps mirror the wider group of more experienced practitioners within the sector.

Trainees often make a distinction between creative teaching and creative learning. Common themes that emerge from the trainees' discussions about creativity include:

- Thinking outside the box
- Doing things differently
- Problem solving
- Taking risks
- Alternative approaches
- Artistic – using music, drawing, painting
- Opening up minds
- Exploring.

Trainees also identify problems and barriers which they associate with using creative approaches in their practice. These typically include:

- 'I'm not a creative person.'
- 'I don't have enough time.'
- 'There are too many pressures to get through with curriculum and assessment.'
- 'The learners don't like it. They just want the easy option. They just want to get through their assignments.'
- 'Other teachers I work with don't do it this way.'
- 'I don't think you can be creative with my subject specialism.'
- 'It's OK for primary schools but I'm not sure how adults and young people would react.'
- 'I just can't come up with the ideas.'

So, creativity might be to do with teaching and the resources or techniques that a teacher chooses to use. They may choose that approach in order to scaffold learning, anticipating potential problem areas which might prove challenging for learners. They may include activities to stimulate learners, to create an impact and to reinforce particular teaching and learning points. For some teachers, creating resources can indeed be problematic if they feel bereft of ideas, inspiration and time to prepare appropriate activities and materials. This is often the case for new teachers who may not have a store of materials to draw upon. Equally, trainees and other more experienced practitioners may have additional and pressing demands on their time or be teaching in challenging environments with limited resources. The ideas in this book may help to provide something of a catalyst for new ideas and at the same time support busy practitioners who are interested in trying out new approaches and techniques.

As the trainees at Huddersfield suggest, 'creativity' is also about learning. Providing learners with the opportunity to explore, to 'think outside the box' and to take responsibility for their own learning can be exciting and liberating but at the same time it is likely to involve a degree of risk taking. It may leave a lesson open-ended. It might take both teachers and learners down unexpected routes. Where assessment and achievement of results in teaching and learning are a priority, introducing an element of uncertainty may leave teachers and learners feeling exposed. Learners may have become used to being told, view the teacher as 'the expert' and may not value their own ideas sufficiently. Teachers and learners may be reluctant in case the approaches are seen as not age-appropriate. Any or all of these may resonate with your situation and that of your learners. To a degree, these issues are more to do with culture and values, including those of teachers and learners, which, by implication, are not as easily solved in a book such as this. They are nonetheless important considerations for practitioners to reflect upon and Part II of the book explores the theoretical and sometimes contentious debates surrounding issues of creativity and innovation in teaching and learning. This is seen to be important to contextualize practical creative teaching within the pedagogical, philosophical and social paradigms of creative thinking.

Part I offers 50 practical and exciting ideas about how creativity might be enhanced in an educational setting. The activities are explained and are intended to act as a catalyst for use and adaptation in different settings. Some activities are short and easy to prepare. Their simplicity, however, should not disguise the potential they may offer as important ways of enhancing teaching or supporting learning. Other activities require more preparation or may involve more time to implement, in some cases over several lessons.

Each activity is arranged in sections. All of the activities begin with a brief rationale which provides you with a précis of the thinking which underpins the approach. It is important that you consider the reason for using a particular approach; the activities are not designed to simply 'fill up a lesson' or to keep learners occupied – 'busyness' does not always equate with learning! The activities vary in their approach and techniques for instance, 'Film Festival', 'Speed Networking' and 'Learning Café' are whole-class exercises involving everyone. 'Radio Interviews', 'Explain to the Aliens' and 'Learning Carousel' focus on group work and others, such as 'Learning Ladders' and 'Using Models and Metaphors', can be used with individual learners. Some activities combine group and individual tasks which may provide variety and interest throughout a session.

Depending on the nature of the activity, it will then be broken down into various sub-headings which might include some or all of the following:

- **What to do**: a step-by-step guide to the way you might use the approach with learners.
- **Practical tips**: includes some helpful suggestions which might help you get the most from the approach. These points often emerge from experience where the authors have used the techniques with their own learners.
- **Danger points**: included here are any essential health and safety considerations which would need to be taken into account, together with suggestions which might forestall possible problems or difficulties.
- **Variations**: ideas as to how the approach could be adapted or taken further.
- **Subject specialist examples**: shows how the activity could be applied within the context of a particular subject specialist area or specific aspect of a course. This section is intended to show just

some of the possibilities and hopefully will leave the way open for you to take the ideas and tailor them for use with a whole range of different courses and learner groups.

- **Thinking points**: this section is aimed at you, the reader. It offers one or two points for reflection which arise out of the suggested approach. It could be to do with the activity itself and the way in which you apply it. Alternatively, it might encourage you to consider wider issues arising from the principles or theoretical ideas which relate to it.
- **What next?**: this section provides signposts to further reading or sources of information which the authors have identified as useful pointers towards further relevant information and ideas.

Part II addresses the theoretical, philosophical, social, and often contentious debates surrounding creativity and innovation in teaching and learning.

The book can be read from cover to cover or more likely 'dipped into' by a wide variety of people involved in teaching and learning. These might include:

- trainee teachers who want to develop and experiment with creative teaching and learning activities within their teaching practice placements;
- newly qualified teachers who need to prepare creative materials for their subject specialist area;
- experienced teachers who are looking for creative ideas to try out with their learners. Developing new strategies could also contribute to their own professional interest and Continuing Professional Development;
- teacher trainers who want to extend their own repertoire of approaches in order to share and model them with their trainees;
- advanced skills teachers who were looking for ideas to improve their own practice, to help advise and mentor other staff;
- trainers who want to use creative techniques within a training or work-based learning environment.

The ideas and activities provided in this book will hopefully allow teachers to further enhance their creative and innovative approaches to their teaching and learning, while at the same time enable them to engage with debates surrounding relevant and important research and theoretical knowledge.

PART I
Practical Activities

1 Text-Free Teaching

Teaching without using text can be challenging but also powerful. Learners are surrounded by a sophisticated visual world and many go into 'switch off' mode when faced with words and text, while learners with literacy difficulties may be particularly challenged. Learners in vocational areas may have difficulty in linking the work they do in theory sessions to the practice of the subject area or the workplace. For many, a picture *is* worth a thousand words. This activity encourages the replacement of words and text with pictures, photographs and other images. Teaching purely with images can make your lessons more interesting for all concerned – as you cannot resort to just reading the content of your visual aids to a class.

What to do

1 Select a lesson which you have previously taught in a traditional way using mainly written forms of communication.
2 Consider how specific sections and content can be replaced by an image. This may be a literal representation or a metaphorical representation to symbolise a point.

Practical tips

- Images can be inserted into presentation software such as PowerPoint.
- Images can be shown one at a time or together in a timed sequence.
- A series of images in a planned sequence can be effective.
- Images set to carefully chosen music will make a lesson a multi-sensory experience.
- Teachers can talk to explain and expand on the images or students can be asked for their interpretation. This can be both interesting and revealing, often giving greater insight into learners' minds – their ideas, perception and ability to make links with previous learning.
- If rooms do not have projection facilities, sets of images can be printed out and laminated for groups to use.
- Collect a series of photographs, postcards or magazine illustrations to provide a resource bank. Differentiation can be achieved by using the same photographs but different questions.
- Laminated and numbered photographs can be used for problem solving, for example, learners could identify what action should be taken when presented with a picture of a skin disorder.

! Danger points

- It can be alarming to take the 'security blanket' of the teacher text away from a lesson! Therefore, start small! Just take one point, concept or section of a lesson to begin with.
- If you are brave enough to teach a whole lesson through images only, it can be reassuring for both teacher and learner to have reference handouts available at end.
- Learners may not 'see the point' and may need to be briefed about the value of learning through images.
- Check your organization's copyright agreements and seek advice. There may be copyright restrictions on images and photographs you may want to use, particularly from the internet.
- If you or your learners take any photographs of other people, it is likely that consent will need to be obtained.

Variations

- Show a sequence of images in a looped presentation before the lesson starts, as students enter. This makes use of 'dead time', providing a visual focus and encouraging interest in the lesson to come.
- Show a sequence of images at the beginning of the lesson as part of your introduction.
- Show selected images at the end of a lesson to consolidate learning. Ask learners to interpret and give feedback.
- Make an instant gallery – pin groups of images in clusters or in a linear sequence for students to look at individually, in pairs or in groups, circulating the room.
- Tremendous impact can be made by using photographs which you or your students have taken.
- A 'lucky dip' activity can be produced by having two boxes, one of photographs and one of generic questions, for example, who, what, where and so on. Learners select an unseen picture and then an unseen question card. The learner then shares their answer with the group.

Subject specialist examples

- *Business Studies* – learners could 'mock up' a product, photograph it and write a marketing piece for the product.
- *Dance and Drama* – learners can select one or several random images which are then interpreted by mime or movement.
- *English* – random images are given to students from which they have to develop a piece of creative writing. A 'lucky dip' system could be used for allocation, for example, a learner picks two images out a bag.
- *ESOL* – learners are asked to produce a visual map using a series of images or photographs of

local landmarks such as the doctor's surgery, the town hall and the supermarket. Working in pairs, the learners then use their maps to practise their communication skills.

- *Hair and Beauty* – learners could consider photographs of current 'celebrity' faces and identify products and techniques which could be used to achieve 'the look'.
- *Leisure Studies* – learners studying holiday venues in a particular area could be given various photographs representing client groups within the industry, for example; a family group, a group of older teenagers, two adults and explore the options for their given group.
- *SLDD* – learners may be taught skills acquisition by breaking the skill down into its component parts. Students with learning difficulties can be provided with photographs and images representing those parts, for example, 'making a sandwich', 'cleaning your teeth' and 'setting a table'.
- *Sport* – learners analyse a series of photographs of different sporting activities and identify the prime energy system being utilized and examples of extension/hyperextension/flexion.
- *Work-based learning* – learners are provided with photographs of work-based settings and are asked to carry out a risk assessment based on their given picture. This might be particularly appropriate for learners on vocational courses (hairdressing salons, construction sites, kitchens) or subjects with a work-based component (science labs, engineering site, care environments).

What next?

Caviglioni, O., Harris, I. and Tindall, B. (2002) *Thinking Skills and EyeQ: Visual Tools for Raising Intelligence.* Stafford: Network Educational Press. This book contains ideas and guidance on using tools such as mind mapping and graphic organisers.

It has been argued that presentation software such as PowerPoint elevates 'format over content', levelling textual information into a series of uniform bullet points. The implications of this are discussed in:

Adams, C. (2006) PowerPoint, habits of mind and classroom culture, *Journal of Curriculum Studies*, 38(4): 389–411.

Colleges and other educational organizations often subscribe to online image banks and these can be useful, copyright-free, searchable sources.

2   Radio Interviews

This activity could be used to encourage learners to become 'expert' in a topic or to present a particular viewpoint on a controversial subject of current interest. While learners will be learning about a specialist topic they will also have the opportunity to develop transferable skills such as verbal communication, question and answer technique and self-confidence.

What to do

1   Learners are going to be asked to prepare for a 'radio interview'. They will need to research the topic and prepare for the interview in advance. The learners will also be asked to take on a specific role during the interview, such as:
    - an 'expert'
    - an advocate for a particular viewpoint
    - the interviewer.
2   On the day, prepare the room so that it looks like a radio studio – chairs, a desk, recording equipment.
3   Role play the interview to a given time scale. The interviewer will be responsible for managing the time available and for bringing the interview to a close.

! Danger points

- Some learners may initially feel intimidated so it will be important to consider how challenging you will make the environment. Some groups will respond best with a small-scale interview, others will enjoy the 'bigger stage' where they have to face a larger audience or deal with challenging or even hostile questions and interviewers!

Variations

- Encourage learners to adopt the opposite position to their own personal viewpoint.
- Make a video recording of the interviews for learners to use for peer or self-assessment.
- A radio 'phone-in' where learners call in and 'ask the experts' or challenge a particular point of view. Providing telephones as props can be helpful.

- Invite an 'audience' which could be made up of other groups of learners or tutors who have not been involved with the preparatory research. They can be invited to question the 'experts'.
- Some computers and laptops come supplied with a built-in video camera. These could be used by pairs of students to conduct their interview which could then be played back to themselves or a larger group for review. This approach may be less intimidating for learners who are less confident.
- Digital video clips can be edited and several interviews compiled to represent the efforts of the whole group.
- If you have a media department in your college, explore the potential for developing links with their staff and students.
- Find out if there is a local radio station in the area and look for possibilities of using their staff and expertise. It may be possible to organise a visit or invite representatives from the radio station to work with the students. Hospital radio may also be a possibility.

Subject specialist examples

- *Applied Science* – the focus of the radio interview centres on a discussion about the proposal for a wind farm development on a site of 'Outstanding Natural Beauty'.
- *Art and Design* – set up a discussion about the Turner Prize, which is well known for controversy.
- *Drama* – it might be particularly helpful to assist learners in developing their vocal technique and devising and using scripts.
- *Health and Social Care* – the proposal that free health care should be means tested.
- *SLDD* – the activity could be used to familiarize learners with using a telephone and to help them to develop questioning and listening skills.

Thinking points

Which transferable skills might a learner develop through engaging with this type of activity?

3   Who Do You Think You Are?

This activity aims to support learners in developing an individual viewpoint or perspective. This encourages learners to think for themselves rather than copy the ideas of their peers. Learners will each be given a scenario, each varying slightly in its detail, to check their understanding and application of the topic.

What to do

1   Provide each learner with a different coloured animal to represent a particular scenario. These animals could be represented on cards or as foam or plastic models. For example, in a Business Studies lesson, the tigers could be sole trader businesses, the lions could be partnerships and the elephants could be limited companies.

2   Make the animals different colours to represent different varieties of businesses. For example, a red animal could be a clothes shop, a blue one could be a restaurant and so on. This would give each learner a separate variety of business within the different type of ownership which they could relate to a particular problem or scenario.

3   Join groups of learners with the same animal. For example, tigers representing sole traders could compare and contrast their results for the different variety of businesses to see how they differ. This could be a sole trader clothes shop compared to a restaurant or a plumber.

4   Move the groups and put the same colour animals together. This time the learners could compare how the same variety of businesses, for example, clothes shops, differed when the ownership altered from, say, a sole trader to a limited company. As each learner has a different coloured animal, they will have to think for themselves about the business they represent.

Practical tips

- As a tutor, it may help to select which animal you give to each learner. This way there can be differentiation between different abilities, giving harder scenarios to the more able ones.

Variations

- These animals can be easily applied to different scenarios, such as issues of diversity and inclusion. The animals could represent different age groups, for example, tigers could be 16–19-year-olds and lions could be 20–35-year-olds. The colours could represent different characteristics, for example, red could be a single parent and blue could be someone from an ethnic minority.

- Learners could research their 'character' using information from the internet, newspaper articles and textbooks.
- A 'Guess Who' game could be played in groups, where the others ask questions to find out about the 'character' and then keep a record of the differences and similarities between them which can be mapped for reference.
- Learners could research their particular 'animal' to become an expert about their topic. The whole group could then share their findings with the others in class by delivering a short presentation.
- If the learner's scenario represented a person, For example, a single teenage mother, the role could be researched and then 'in character' contribute to a discussion panel around a particular topic to create a lively debate.

Subject specialist examples

- *Art and Design* – schools of artists teaching different subjects.
- *Health and Social Care* – the animal which the learner is given could represent patients with different illnesses or, alternatively, their animal represents a particular individual with specified characteristics or personal circumstances. In the latter scenario, the group would all consider the same illness, but from different perspectives according to their given cameo.

4 Dominoes

 Effective recap and reinforcement is a feature of good learning. Playing dominoes provides a visual and kinaesthetic opportunity to consolidate learning points. Students can work singly, in pairs or in small groups. Peer teaching can be developed within groups and pairs. Checking of the finished game provides reinforcement of correct answers.

The technique can be used across all academic levels and subjects.

What to do

1 Prepare between 15 and 30 mix and match questions (although this number will vary according to subject and student need).
2 Prepare a template using the table facility on your computer similar to the one shown in Figure 4.1. Input your questions and answers as on the template, ensuring that your first domino begins with a shaded area and that the final one ends with a shaded area.

Start	Question A
Answer A	Question B
Answer B	Question C
Answer C	Question D
Answer D	Finish

Figure 4.1

3 Produce an additional copy to use as a model answer.
4 Cut out your completed dominoes from the template, *along the horizontals only*. Take care not to cut your dominoes in half!
5 To play the game, place the start domino (with the blank left side) in the centre of the table and divide the rest of the dominoes between the learners in their pairs/groups. If learners are playing singly, they will have all the dominoes.
6 Learners then add a relevant domino to the start domino making either a square or a long line to complete the sequence.
7 When learners indicate that they have completed the activity ask another learner to check against the model answer.

Practical tips

- Circulate as the activity is undertaken to identify areas of misunderstanding.
- If you are making several sets, choose different colours to make sorting easy.
- Ensure that there are no questions which could be satisfied by several of the answer blocks.
- If learners produce their own dominoes (see variation below), ask them to provide you with a completed electronic copy of their template. This adds to your resource bank!
- Textured dominoes can be helpful to learners with visual impairments.
- Have some pointers to source texts, if appropriate, on the reverse of the dominoes. This enables learners to research areas of difficulty at their leisure.

Variations

- Use the dominoes as a mix and match activity using images rather than text. For example, in *SLDD*, a learner boiling vegetables can match pictures of commodity and equipment.
- Large dominoes can be used on the floor, providing there is sufficient space.
- Use a set of floor dominoes to make an attractive frieze in a base room.
- Ask learners to prepare a set of dominoes on an area they found difficult for the next group.
- A larger set with more questions can be used as a whole-class activity. Provide each learner with one or more dominoes to ensure full participation.
- Learners could form a human chain by positioning themselves in the correct sequence.
- The original template could be used to provide focus for a key word activity. Cut each domino in half to produce sets of cards.
- Learners select a card from a top hat or bag and talk about the subject on the card for 30 seconds.
- Learners can use the dominoes as a verbal activity. Each learner has a domino and the person with the starter domino reads out the question. The learner who has the answer reads it out and then asks the next question. Learners can be timed doing this exercise and, if they go wrong, have to start again. This can be used as a regular recap activity, as each time the learner will receive a different domino.

Subject specialist examples

Topics which might be suitable for creating sets of dominoes include:

- *Business Studies* – accountancy terms and definitions.
- *Chemistry* – elements and compounds.
- *Construction* – built environment terms and practice.
- *Science* – anatomy and physiology of the digestive process.
- *Social Sciences* – the principles of psychological learning theories.

5 In the Bag

Learners can sometimes find it difficult to articulate concepts and ideas in writing and other conventional ways. This activity asks learners to place objects which they think represent or symbolise concepts or ideas associated with a topic in a bag. Learners then present the bag and its contents, explaining reasons for their choices. Some learners can find it easier to present to a group if they have something to hold, show and 'talk around'. The exercise promotes differentiation through task outcome and enables the teacher to assess knowledge and understanding through the choice of objects and accompanying presentation.

What to do

1   Ask learners to select five or seven objects which represent a chosen topic or theme and to put them in a bag, for example, learners could be asked to select items which represent 'Professionalism'. The interpretation may be literal, for example, a clock could represent 'time management'. However, higher level learners might be encouraged to provide a more metaphorical representation, for example, the clock could represent the chronological development of a profession and the corresponding challenges for the professional.

2   Give the learners an example to prevent misunderstandings.
3   Set a date for learners to present their chosen items to the whole class.

! Danger points

- Learners for whom English is not their first language may struggle with the concept of representation and metaphor. Completing the task with a learning partner may be helpful.

Variations

- The bag itself may also represent or symbolise an idea. Ask learners to consider this.
- Ask learners to develop their ideas into an essay, writing a paragraph about each item.
- Develop self-, peer and teacher evaluation sheets.
- Learners on higher level courses can be asked to link each item to a particular theory or an academic reference.
- Learners could be asked to select and plan for the objects to be presented to a specific audience, for example, children or parents.

- Learners could research independently before their presentation as a starting point for a topic or the task could follow teaching and learning and be used to consolidate.
- The teacher provides a selection of items and learners consider, as a class or in small groups, what they may represent.
- Rather than using real objects, some learners may be able to meet the challenge of producing a digital presentation in which the chosen bags and objects are animated or have an interactive interface. This could provide a further opportunity for learners to share their ideas through the internet or a web-based platform.

Subject specialist examples

Listed below are some topics which might lend themselves to this approach:

- *Art and Design* – historical movements such as Surrealism, Dadaism.
- *Business Studies* – features of a well-run business.
- *Entry to Employment* – principles of effective communication.
- *Health and Social Care* – effective supervision.
- *Social Sciences* – key theories in sociology, psychology, child development.
- *Teacher Education* – the concept of professionalism.
- *Travel and Tourism* – customer care.

6 Using Models and Metaphors

Communication through the use of models or metaphors can be an effective tool in helping learners to express their ideas or to explore complex or sensitive issues. It is likely to appeal particularly to learners who enjoy visual and/or kinaesthetic learning.

Learners often have to explore ideas and concepts which are not easily defined or are open to interpretation. We often ask learners to write down or tell us '... In your own words, what do you understand by ...' Some learners might find this difficult in the first instance, however, by creating a model and talking through what it represents, this can be a useful starting point. The process of explaining allows the learner to articulate and refine their ideas.

This technique has many applications. Learners might find it helpful to produce a model which represents their initial ideas for a project or presentation. It is also good for exploring experiences, for example, the learner's perception of themselves within a team, an organization or a work placement. Learners could model their perception of how things are and then how the learner might like them to be at some point in the future, which would then open up the discussion as to how they might achieve that position and any barriers that might exist. This would link with personal and professional development plans and tutorials.

Many courses now require learners to engage in reflective practice and metaphorical modelling can be a useful tool in facilitating that process.

What to do

1   Choose a medium for learners to work with. Things you might consider using include:
    - building bricks
    - play dough
    - drinking straws and sticky notes
    - pipe cleaners.
2   Set up the room so that there is sufficient space for learners to work and move around and ensure that all learners have access to a full range of materials.
3   Explain the purpose of the activity to the learners.
4   Ask learners to produce a model which represents their ideas, using the materials provided. It is best to encourage learners to produce their own individual work. See Figures 6.1 and 6.2 for examples.
5   Learners then use the model as a prompt to explain their thinking. This can be to the rest of the group, a small group or one-to-one.

Figures 6.1 and 6.2

Practical tips

- It is important to allow learners the freedom to express their ideas in their own way and not to impose or correct.
- Some learners might feel inhibited to begin with so it is important to build in some 'play time' to give the opportunity to get to experiment with the materials.
- Consider the use of background music while learners are working on producing their models. Changing the volume of the music can be used to signal the timing of the activity or to bring the group back together. This can often be less imposing and more effective than relying on the teacher's voice.
- It is important that the learners are encouraged to take ownership of their model and so the role of the teacher should be very much that of facilitator, with as little direction as possible.
- Treat the models with respect: the learner may get very attached to their model so it is a good idea to offer them a photograph or video recording.
- Think about how the models will be dismantled at the end of the session.
- Allow sufficient time for the model building and the feedback/discussion phase.
- The technique will probably work best with small groups as the feedback and discussion arising from each model can be quite lengthy and individuals need to feel they have sufficient time to share their ideas.

Variations

- Learners could be asked to explore aspects of their model in more detail. This can be done by taking one feature and building a further model which represents macro or micro aspects. This can also be helpful when a learner completes the original task much more quickly than others in the group.
- Take a photograph of the models and return to the pictures at a later date to discuss and review.
- With the permission of the learners you might consider taking digital photographs of their models which could then be incorporated into PowerPoint presentations, learners' work,

their reflective journals or their e-portfolios. You could also use them as examples of completed work for other groups at the start of their activity.

- Not all teachers may have access to modelling resources, but paper, scissors and glue can be used to create simple models, origami style!

Subject specialist examples

- *Business Studies* – models which represent management systems, organizational structures and cultures, team working and communications within businesses.
- *Health and Social Care* – learners build a model to represent their work placement and their role within it. It can be particularly helpful in describing their role within the placement and the working relationships they are developing between staff and clients at the placement.
- *Personal Development Planning* – models can be used to represent personal development on a course – progress, barriers and aspirations. This might be particularly appropriate in tutorial sessions.
- *Planning for Projects* – a model that represents how a learner proposes to tackle a presentation, assignment or dissertation.
- *Tutorials* – a model which expresses how that learner perceives the tutor group and their place within it. This could be helpful in addressing group dynamics and classroom management issues.

Thinking points

This approach could be valuable in tackling personal or sensitive issues with groups of learners. What are the implications for the tutor in preparing and running such a session?

What next?

'Lego Serious Play' is a part of the Lego group and pioneered the application of creative techniques, building and metaphor to a range of business and educational contexts. Further detail of this work can be found on the Lego Serious Play website at http://www.seriousplay.com.

A very readable text by Professor David Gauntlett, exploring the use of visual and creative methods would be useful follow-up reading: Gauntlett, D. (2007) *Creative Explorations: New Approaches to Identities and Audiences*. Abingdon: Routledge.

To read more about the use of metaphors in everyday life and thinking: Lakeoff, G. and Johnson, M. (1980) *Metaphors We Live By*. Chicago: University of Chicago Press.

7　The Learning Café

Using a theme for the lesson can bring a 'fun' element into the learning activities. The café theme is an excellent way to get learners networking and sharing ideas in an informal, but structured way. This encourages collaboration between them and the development of new approaches to problems which everyone can chew through. It could be an ideal activity for learners who do not know each other beforehand.

What to do

1   Before the session starts, the tables need to be arranged in 'bistro' style, so that approximately six people can sit around each one. Lay coloured tablecloths on each table.
2   Use numbered wooden spoons, different coloured candles or flowers in wine bottles to divide the groups up into assorted interests.
3   Allocate a 'waiter' to each table whose function is to facilitate, record and summarise feedback from discussions. If the 'waiters' are allocated their role before the session, they can dress for the part to add to the theme, for example, they could wear white tops and black trousers.
4   If the learners or, in this case 'diners', do not know each other well, give them a name label and encourage them to sit on a table with others they do not know. A more diverse and interesting set of results will emerge in this way.
5   Make it a rule that the 'diners' must make at least one new contact with whom they can collaborate after the session.
6   Give each group a different aspect of the topic to discuss in an allocated time. The waiter records the information on flipchart paper as words, drawings or diagrams.
7   When time is up, the 'waiters' should stay at their table, but each 'diner' should move to a different table making sure that they sit with a new group of people.
8   The waiter now facilitates discussion on the same theme, but with the new set of diners.
9   Moving the 'diners' three times is usually enough. The tutor then invites the waiters to feed back a summary of the findings.

Practical tips

- Paper tablecloths can be used to 'spill' and capture ideas. Alternatively, flipchart paper can be used as a cheaper option.
- In a large group, replication of some of the table themes will allow all learners to make a contribution to each topic.

- Ensure enough time is allowed for each question, so that the 'diners' have the space and time to share their ideas.
- Provide the participants with 'business cards' so that it is easy to follow up a new contact.
- The waiters could be responsible for collating the ideas in writing and circulating them to the group.

Variations

- Different themes such as a party or a dinner dance could be used.
- Arrange for 'experts' to give a brief talk before the café starts. These 'experts' could then be the waiters on the tables to help facilitate discussion.
- A 'tips' box could be kept in the room for new ideas.
- A 'menu' with 'starters and puddings', 'today's specials' and 'after-dinner mints' can be prepared in place of an agenda or task sheet!
- Learners could undertake the activity in pairs. A task or key words could be presented on a customised handout, which they could discuss 'over coffee'.
- Learners could be actively involved in setting up the learning café themselves and organise the activities.

Subject specialist examples

- *Business Studies* – each table could consider how to improve the functions of different departments within an organization, such as sales, production and personnel.
- *Early Years* – play for different stages of child development where each table would represent a different age group.
- *Health and Social Care* – prioritising the allocation of resources and services for different clients being cared for within the community.
- *Public Services* – exploring the preparation and planning necessary to support the management of a major public event, such as a music festival, protest march or charity run.

8   On the One Hand

 Some learners may find it difficult to marshal their thoughts to structure a piece of writing which demands an element of reasoning. This kinaesthetic activity allows for a 'breathing space' in a session, enabling learners to work at their own pace and think through their ideas. Problem-solving scenarios can be introduced and a course of action evaluated in a fun way. It can also be used to encourage learners to consider issues from different perspectives or to formulate or construct an argument.

What to do

1   Provide each learner with two differently coloured pieces of card, a felt tip pen and a pair of scissors.
2   The learner draws round their left hand on one piece of card and their right hand on the other.
3   The learner cuts out the hand shapes.
4   Present a scenario to the learner and ask them to identify 'for' points on one hand, one point per digit, and 'against' points on the other hand
5   Use the points identified to provide the basis for a group discussion or as a foundation for planning individual work.

Practical tips

- Use different colours of card for each hand.
- Provide left-handed scissors, if appropriate.

! Danger points

- If you have learners with limited coordination, it would be advisable to use commercial sticky gum to hold down card for learners when drawing round their hands.
- Paper rather than card may be easier to cut for some learners.
- Omit the cutting-out stage or have pre-cut hand shapes for learners for whom the use of scissors is difficult.
- Remember to check numbers of scissors collected in at the end of the session.

Variations

- Introduce 'helping hands' for a topic. Provide one set of helping hands cards for each topic which are kept in a central location within the classroom. These will identify key points and can be used as necessary by the learner for providing structure either during the task or as self-assessment on completion.
- Use footprints instead of handprints. Module requirements can be identified and used as a frieze around the learning space forming a 'success path'.
- Copies of completed prints can be saved for revision or display material.
- Provide a footprint path for a course. Learners can be 'walked' along the path during induction.
- Footprints can be used to break down stages in a new concept.
- Small, pre-prepared feet cards can record learners' progress towards their individual learning plans.

Subject specialist examples

- *Entry to Employment* – learners can consider personal skills against job specifications.
- *Hair and Beauty* – learners can compare permanent and semi-permanent colouring techniques.
- *ICT* – learners can compare the advantages and limitations of two software packages.
- *Law* – key points of advice which could be offered to a client.
- *SLDD* – learners can use one hand to identify key features of personal hygiene.

Thinking points

Think of a group of learners you regularly teach. What are the possible benefits and limitations of using kinaesthetic activities with those learners?

9   Learning Laundry Line

 Using a washing line for learning to be 'pegged out' can be helpful for visual and kinaesthetic learners. It can help learners to understand key concepts and construct personal meaning. Active and collaborative learning is promoted by this activity which requires learners to work away from desks and move around while working with others.

Laundry lines can be very useful in helping learners to 'construct and crystallize' their understanding. For example, things that are easily understood can be easily placed on a line. Those that are harder to place may suggest that further learning activities and clarification are needed. Continuum lines can highlight 'grey' areas in the middle and this can promote interesting and useful discussion.

What to do

1   Prepare a set of cards with key words which are associated with a chosen topic. Select key words, key names, key phrases, representative images and dates (if appropriate).
2   Erect a washing/laundry line between two fixed points in the classroom, paying attention to health and safety.
3   Mix and share out the cards between all the learners. Give each learner a handful of pegs.
4   Ask all learners to 'peg' their cards onto the laundry line grouping them into related and linked sections. Ask them to talk and justify their decisions as they work.
5   Give out a handout which covers all the key information – and ask if they need to re-arrange anything on the line as a result.

! Danger points

- Health and safety – if you are using a long line you will need to think carefully about where you will place it within the classroom. Take care that learners can reach it comfortably and that it does not obstruct free movement around the room – especially access to exits.

Variations

- Timeline activity – learners have to arrange dates in correct chronological order.
- Continuum – learners have to arrange cards using the laundry line as a continuum.
- Sequence – learners have to arrange cards in a correct sequence.
- Competition – two washing lines with two groups working in competition to place cards in

the correct order. Each group works out of sight of the other group. Compare and contrast the two results on both lines.

- Images or symbols are used on some cards to represent key words or concepts.

Subject specialist examples

- *Accounting* – the sequence of a business document, for example, a purchase order being processed through the book-keeping system.
- *Art and Design* – create a timeline of art movements with key dates and representative images.
- *Business Administration* – a key procedure such as the recruitment and induction of new staff, to be sequenced correctly creating a visual flow chart.
- *Drugs Awareness* – create a continuum with 'hard' and 'soft' at opposite ends of the washing line. Learners have to place cards with drug names on the line.
- *Early Years* – stages in child development could be placed in correct sequential order.
- *Science* – create the different stages of reactions or processes, for example, photosynthesis.
- *SLDD* – using picture cards or shaped templates (for example, plates, cutlery and so on), learners running a snack bar can sequence the order of preparations.
- *Social Sciences* – key learning theories to be grouped into a timeline with key names, concepts, terms and representative images (for example, an image of a dog and a bell to represent Pavlov).

What next?

The laundry lines make use of different senses. Have a look at this article about Howard Gardner's ideas: http://www.infed.org/thinkers/gardner.htm.

When you have tried out the activity with your learners and having read the article, reflect on how Gardner's thinking relates to learning with laundry lines!

10 Terminology Bingo

In most specialist subject areas, learners will need to be able to recognise and use unfamiliar language and terminology. Using the senses in different ways can help to reinforce new words and phrases; sight, hearing and speaking in particular.

If a word or phrase is only used once, it is likely to be forgotten. Repetition is important in the learning process and introducing the terminology in different ways within a lesson can be very helpful to learners.

Learners can sometimes feel daunted by unfamiliar terminology and lack confidence in using it. Using interesting and fun ways to enable learners to use and 'play' with terminology can help them to become more confident in understanding the language and using it appropriately.

What to do

1   At the start of the lesson each learner is given a bingo card which includes key words or terms they will hear used by the teacher during the session.
2   When the learner hears the teacher say a word which appears on their card during the lesson, they mark off the corresponding word on their bingo card.
3   The winner is the first learner to call out 'BINGO' having ticked off all the terms on their bingo card.
4   Before any 'prize' is awarded, the card should be checked. This can be another opportunity for the teacher to ask questions of the group about each item and so further consolidate the learning.

Variations

- First learner to complete a single line or the four corners on the card.
- The winner has to provide a sentence which makes correct use of one of the terms on the card.
- Learners have to find the words on their cards by looking at books, websites, handouts provided.
- Words are drawn at random (in bingo style) from a box as part of the review and recap at the end of a session.
- Images are used on the card to represent key words.
- If delivering a lecture to a large group of learners, design the bingo cards so there is one word common to all cards which is not said until the very end of the lecture. If it works, everyone will shout 'BINGO' at the same time – and their attention will be guaranteed until the end of the lecture!
- Ask learners to mark points on their card as they are observing a video clip. They can be asked to explain their responses.

Subject specialist examples

- *Accounting* – accounting terms on a set of final accounts.
- *Anatomy and Physiology* – learners learning about the circulatory system (see Figure 10.1).
- *Nutrition* – macro and micro nutrients.
- *Sports Science* – introduction to the main muscles in biomechanics.

Myocardium	Aorta	Tricuspid valve	Capillaries
Aortic valve	Heart		Oxygenated
	Left ventricle	Left Lung	Pulmonary vein
Right Lung	Deoxygenated	Carbon dioxide	Oxygen

Figure 10.1

Thinking points

Think of a topic you teach and add your own key words or new terms to the template in Figure 10.2.

Figure 10.2

11 A Card to Remember

Postcards or greetings cards can be used at the end of a project, module or course to help build self-esteem in a learner and build positive relationships with others in the group. Regardless of subject specialism or academic level, it is not unusual to find that learners within the post-compulsory sector in particular, often lack confidence and self-esteem which in turn can impact upon their achievement and interpersonal skills. This activity gives all the learners a 'feel good' factor at the end of the session and some positive thoughts to take away with them. The cards might also promote self-evaluation and reflection into areas for personal development.

What to do

1   At the end of the module or course, the tutor prepares a personal card for every learner. On one side of the card is written *'Thank you for . . .'* and on the other side of the card is written *'I would like you to . . .'*
2   Before the session the tutor enters the first comment so that the card has a positive statement at the top.
3   Once learners have received their cards from the tutor, the cards are circulated and completed by other group members.
4   When all the cards are completed, they are handed back to the individual learner and the group sit round in a circle. Each learner is given a clip or peg (if novelty ones are available, even better).
5   A person then has to stand up and the person to the left of them clips the card on them as a 'medal'. As they do so, they read out one positive statement from the card. The 'medal' ceremony is then continued around the room, until everyone is wearing a 'medal'.

! Danger points

- If this exercise is being used to convey personal thoughts, the tutor may need to supervise carefully as some of the participants might try and spoil the spirit of the activity by including inappropriate or hurtful comments.
- The use of *positive* comments must be stressed.

Variations

- Some learners might find it helpful to have access to sample phrases or feedback sentence beginnings.
- A similar exercise can be done using postcards. On one side can be written *'I appreciate . . .'* and on the other *'The gift I would give you is . . .'*. This version could be used where the focus of the course has been personal and effective learning, for example, in a counselling or tutor group.
- Ask learners to design a greetings card to send to another person in the group. This card should express what they have valued about them in the class.
- Have a selection of cards and photos on the table, where each learner selects one to describe the qualities they like about another person in the group, (in some groups this may need some careful allocation by the tutor!)
- The postcards could be used as an evaluation exercise. What was most enjoyable about the topic? Easy to understand? And what elements of it could be improved or were hard to grasp? How could it be improved?
- Learners can follow up and work on some of the developmental points raised by their tutor and peers. These could be reviewed through the tutorial system to help them in their future studies.
- Learners could find their own cards and photos to share and bring them to the lesson.

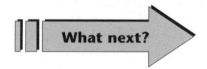

What next?

The principle of using positive and developmental feedback with learners can be followed up in Petty's work using 'medal and mission' (2004: 65). Wallace (2002) illustrates and discusses the usefulness and limitations of various learning theories in relation to motivating learners and encouraging positive behaviour.

References

Petty, G. (2004) *Teaching Today*. Cheltenham: Nelson Thornes.
Wallace, S. (2002) *Managing Behaviour and Motivating Students in Further Education*. Exeter: Learning Matters.

12 Menu Cards

In planning lessons, tutors need to identify key learning points and new vocabulary which the learners will need to assimilate during a session. Frequent recap of key points is vital. This can be achieved through verbal or visual means. This repetition and reinforcement helps to promote familiarity with, and confidence in, using appropriate vocabulary. This also helps to embed new knowledge in the long-term memory. Individualized menus for learners can be provided to aid differentiation.

What to do

1   You will need some place card holders. Alternatively, fold a small piece of strong card in half and make a small incision in the fold. Place the folded edge to the top, providing a stand into which the 'menu' can be slipped.
2   Print new vocabulary on one side of the card, the task or topic on the other.
3   Place a menu on each work area.

Practical tips

- Laminate cards for durability.
- Punch the cards so that they can be easily filed for future reference.

Variations

- Separate a learning task into three courses: starter, main, dessert. This will provide a scaffold to help the learner plan their work. On the back of the card, list suitable books, websites and so on, accompanied by a brief description of their content. This can facilitate development of the topic and provide extension material for some learners.
- Provide the learning outcomes for a task and ask learners to produce their own menu showing what will be required to meet these outcomes. The format for the menu can vary, for example, some learners may prefer to produce text, others may prefer to produce a web page or audiovisual recording.
- A file of skills-related menus can be established listing equipment needed. The appropriate menu card can be collected by the learner before a practical task is commenced.
- Menus could be used to display visual reminders of health and safety points and key instructions to be followed during practical activities, for example, laboratory sessions and built environment workshops.

Subject specialist examples

- *Basic Literacy* – learners can be provided with a menu of tasks and can choose a presentation style from the menu, for example, a newspaper article or a letter or story.
- *Built Environment* – a menu file can be kept in the resource store. Learners can select a menu card associated with mitred joints or using a circuit board as they collect their equipment.
- *Early Years* – a menu relating to preparing a formula feed can be used.
- *Entry to Employment* – learners can select a menu card when producing a speculative job application.
- *Hair and Beauty* – learners can select a menu for a treatment process.

Thinking points

Think of how you could use menu cards to provide differentiation of both task and outcome.

13 Learning Party

Making a lesson into an 'event' can transform an ordinary session into something special. Holding a 'Learning Party' can be one way to celebrate success and achievement while reinforcing and consolidating learning. It is ideal for an end-of-term session or for the end of a unit or module.

What to do

1   Send out invitations (see Figure 13.1).

> *You are invited to a*
> *LEARNING PARTY*
> *Celebrate your learning and achievement*
> *R.S.V.P*

Figure 13.1

2   Publicize the party with posters and flyers to arouse interest and build anticipation.
3   Plan a range of activities adapted from celebratory events and parties. Aim for a varied mix and ensure you start with icebreakers which require 'guests' to circulate and mix. Example activities could include:
  * *Pass the Parcel*: Wrap a small prize in newspaper. In each layer include a question to be answered and a sweet.
  * *Kim's Game*: Small teams compete against each other to remember items on a tray, with the twist that each item represents an aspect of recent learning.
  * *Spot Prize*: Award instant prizes for good responses and contributions throughout the party.
  * *Quiz Time*: Hold a quiz related to previous learning. Plan for learners to find a learning partner or form a team in a fun way.
  * *Star Awards*: Hold a mini prize-giving ceremony for learners who deserve recognition for effort, attitude or achievement.
  * *Guest Speaker*: Invite someone from industry, employment, careers or even your department to give a short motivational talk and to present awards.
  * *Competitions and Challenges*: Devise learning-related activities for pairs or small teams.
4   At the end of the party, give out 'Party Bags' for learners to take as they leave. Fill a carrier bag with a mix of items, some fun and some related to learning. Your organization may have some pens and cheap stationery items left over from open days which they may be willing to give you. If you are lucky, you may be able to get bags which carry your organization logo.

Practical tips

- Use motivational or themed music to create a positive ambience as learners enter the room and during activities.
- Set up quick display materials for the walls – posters, quotations, photographs, etc. and consider themed decorations. Balloons are a quick and inexpensive way to give an instant 'party feel' to an ordinary classroom.
- Contact and ask local organizations and supermarkets to sponsor some small prizes – they often have 'community funds' to enable them to support local initiatives.

Variations

- Learners could be actively involved in the planning and organization of the party themselves.
- Link to a seasonal time of year or a particular cultural or religious celebration, for example:
  - a Chinese New Year theme could be colour-themed with appropriate decorations and include fortune cookies;
  - a Christmas theme could include festive crackers;
  - an event held in the summer could be hosted outdoors as a Garden Party with bunting, lucky dip, strawberries, ice cream.
- The content and party activities could be as easy or as hard and challenging as you make them, for example, party bags for higher level learners could include academic journal articles.

Subject specialist examples

- *Business Studies* – learners can prepare a budget and then research and source items.
- *Drama* – learners can research and attend the party in character; teachers can make links to plays such as Mike Leigh's *Abigail's Party*.
- *SLDD* – hold an Afternoon Tea Party where learners are shown how to set out a table, greet guests, offer and make drinks.

Thinking points

Some learners may not appreciate the learning value of the party. How can you overcome this?

14 Board Games

Board games are adaptable and can provide opportunities for learners to explore topics in many different ways. A simple board game might be used as a fun revision aid but it can also be used to explore complex topics which require higher order thinking skills. It may be used to encourage collaborative learning, competition and exploration of sensitive topics.

This type of activity may be used to revise a topic, as an introduction to a topic, to establish prior knowledge and understanding and in some instances to explore some of the myths or misunderstanding associated with that topic.

What to do

1   Take an A1 piece of thick card or foam board and mark out the perimeter of your board into squares.
2   Mark a **Start** square on your board. It is a good idea to put an arrow on this square which indicates the direction of play around the board.
3   You will need a die and some playing pieces – one piece for each player. The playing pieces could be coloured counters or small objects which are of some significance to the 'topic' you have chosen.
4   Prepare some cards which will be used with the game. As learners progress around the board they will pick up a certain card which links with the square upon which they land. You can create different types of card but the choice will depend on the topic and the learners who will be using the game.
5   Suggestions for card categories you might want to consider (see Figure 14.1) include:
    (a)   Specific questions about a chosen topic
    (b)   True or False cards
    (c)   'What would you do if …?' cards
    (d)   'Advice' cards
    (e)   Multiple choice cards.

Figure 14.1

6   Prepare a 'specimen answer' sheet for the questions.

7   The design of your board is up to you and you can be as creative as you like with the features you include! See Figure 14.2.

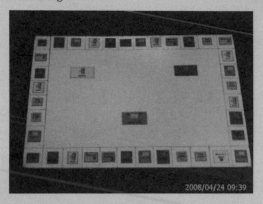

Figure 14.2

8   It is a good idea to design your board so that the same board can be used for different topics using different question banks.

9   You will need to consider how best to organise your learners. If the learners are playing independently, then probably four learners playing one game would be ideal with one other learner to act as judge or referee. That person would also be in charge of the answer sheet!

Practical tips

- Once you have 'road tested' your game and are satisfied with the content, laminate the banks of cards to preserve them and give them a longer shelf life.
- Consider how you constitute the players and teams as the activity offers the potential for different learners to work together.

Variations

- Learners play the game in teams and confer on their answers.
- Learners prepare the playing cards themselves by devising relevant questions and answers. This could be either a useful revision activity or, alternatively, learners research a new topic before compiling a set of questions. The sets of cards which a group of learners produce could then be used by another group to play their game.
- Create an interactive electronic version of your board and display it using PowerPoint or an Interactive Whiteboard. The game could then be played by a larger group.
- Produce differentiated banks of questions for the same topic to cater for learners who might be beginners or more advanced and include both easy and more difficult questions to challenge but also ensure some success. Learners could be grouped accordingly or choose themselves the level of difficulty.

Subject specialist examples

- *Built Environment* – stages in construction, the contribution of differing trades and safety procedures could all be addressed.
- *Early Years* – principles and practice of play with young children is a significant area of learning within this specialism. This would encourage learners to demonstrate their knowledge and understanding of relevant theory and the application to practice in placement.
- *Hair and Beauty* – a board game could be used to reinforce important aspects of relevant processes and contraindications which practitioners will need to be aware of when working with their clients. The board game could be designed to assist with recall of key factual information and also to allow for discussion of application of theory to the workplace.
- *Health and Social Care* – create a board game to help learners to consider and discuss aspects of sexual health. Card sets could include categories such as *'Advice'* and *'What would you do if . . .?'* or *'True and False'* would enable learners to explore a subject and discuss ideas which they might find embarrassing or uncomfortable if taught using a more formal approach.
- *Language Teaching* – principles of correct use of punctuation and specialist terms such as alliteration could be reinforced
- *Law* – exploring topics such as medical negligence or property law. It could include questions relating to factual information and also advice which might be given to clients.
- *SLDD* – learners could learn about safety issues covering home, personal and road safety through playing a game presented in a suitable format.

15 Odd Opposites

 This activity is designed to make learners think creatively about a topic. It encourages them to use the strangest opposites and link them to a topic, thus creating some interesting and different approaches to their work.

What to do

1. Four or five learners are put into a group and given a topic to discuss, for example, '3-D Shapes'. They are then given a pile of cards with a pair of opposite words written on each card. For example, pairs such as: 'Tame or Wild', 'Joy or Sorrow', and 'Asleep or Awake'.
2. Each person has five of these 'opposite' cards and they each select one card (the odder, the better) and put it on the table. Therefore, there will be four or five cards on the table depending on how many are in the group.
3. The group then discuss the topic by trying to link it to each of these 'opposite cards'. Usually, the strangest opposites often give the best results. In this example, the group may discuss 3-D shapes in relation to the 'Joy or Sorrow' card. It is possible that this discussion may lead to an enquiry about 3-D shapes that are pleasing to look at compared to those which are ugly. The 'Asleep or Awake' card could lead to a discussion about shapes that you might ignore or not notice compared to those which startle you or catch your attention and why this is so.
4. Once all the cards have been discussed, the group decide which card has given the most interesting outcomes and the person who has chosen the card is given a point. This process can be repeated with other topics and 'opposite cards'. When all topics have been covered, the learner with the most points is the winner.
5. When the topics have been covered, the ideas raised from the 'opposite' cards can be used and followed up by the learners in their studies.

Practical tips

- Ask the learners to record the ideas they come up with, regardless of how bizarre they might seem. Quite often when they return to their notes, these ideas trigger new thoughts and ideas leading to further interesting developments in their work.

Variations

- This technique could be used by teachers to help provide ideas for lesson planning.
- Try and make links with dissimilar topics. For example, in Sport, find connections between football and tennis.
- Use a table of assorted objects (the more varied the better), to discuss a topic, such as a group of playwrights. Ask the learners to decide which object is the odd one out and does not link to the topic. Links can be made with the most bizarre group of objects and, as a result, these connections may then be better retained in the memory.

Subject specialist examples

- *Art and Design* – ideas to develop the features of a design they are creating.
- *Business Studies* – ideas on how to promote a new product in the marketplace.
- *Drama* – characterisation exercises.
- *Music Technology* – composition experimentation.

16 Get Physical

 This is similar to a well-known party game. Learners can be used to model a product or process; forming interesting shapes adds to the fun. This activity is likely to appeal to learners who find it difficult to sit still throughout the session and can provide an energising few minutes at any stage of the session.

What to do

1 Make a series of A4 labels representing either stages in a process or component parts and attach one label to each learner.
2 Clear a large space, which can be defined by a marked area on the floor.
3 Ask learners to arrange themselves, representing the process and talk about their role within the process.

Practical tips

- Physical contact is useful to underline steps in the process. This can be done by hand holding or making links with string or ribbon.
- Annotated and coloured balloons can be used in place of cards.

! Danger points

- Limit the size of groups to minimize health and safety risks.
- Ensure sufficient space for wheelchair users to engage with the activity.
- Long paper streamers instead of string will make links that can easily be broken if they become trapped in wheelchair mechanics.
- Use sticky tape or commercial sticky gum, rather than pins, to attach labels.
- As this activity involves physical contact, teachers will need to be mindful of gender and cultural sensitivities and provide learners with appropriate reminders.

Variations

- Use as a revision exercise. Divide the class into two teams. Allocate a (secret) topic to each team who agree on the representation of the process.
- The learners then prepare labels for each person and attach them, information facing inwards. The teams take turns in selecting one card to be revealed by the other team and positioning the person wearing it appropriately. An element of competition can be introduced by limiting the time allowed for placing each person.

Subject specialist examples

- *Business Studies* – learners can represent stages in setting up a business or product development.
- *ESOL* – learners can assume a role, for example, an adjective, noun or verb and the group is encouraged to develop a simple narrative.
- *ICT* – learners can represent the components and features of a personal computer.
- *Law* – learners can represent personnel involved in court proceedings.
- *Science* – learners can represent the digestive system, cell membrane function or food webs.

17 Learning Carousel

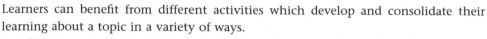

Learners can benefit from different activities which develop and consolidate their learning about a topic in a variety of ways.

Creating a carousel of different activities for learners to move around in one room is a way of maintaining active learning and participation. It can also energize a class as a new activity is undertaken at regular intervals – ideal for after lunch! Working in small groups also promotes collaboration and peer learning. Sometimes a 'review week' can contain dead time; a learning carousel can provide a focus.

What to do

1. Select a topic and devise four different activities which link to the topic. Aim for as much variety as possible.
2. Arrange the classroom into four different 'learning stations' – one in each corner can work well.
3. Split the class into four groups.
4. Allocate each group to a 'learning station' and explain carefully that when you signal, each group is to move clockwise to the next activity.
5. When all groups have visited each station, plan a whole class debrief section, where learning can be consolidated. Follow with a personal review period with time for personal reflection – this contrast is important as the carousel phase will have been very busy and active.

Practical tips

- Plan the timings in advance and share with the learners to ensure that everyone has the opportunity to participate fully in the planned activities.
- Allow sufficient time for review and consolidation of learning at the end of the carousel.
- Consider the make-up of the groups as carousels offer a great opportunity for differentiation.

Variations

Consider a mix of the following activities:

- Mix and match card exercise (for example, classify cards into 'Dos or Don'ts', 'True or False', 'Terms or Definitions').

- Analysis of a key document (for example, reduced to 10 bullet points).
- Case study with questions.
- Competition (for example, how many ways to …?).
- Integration of an exercise using IT facilities if the teaching room has them, for instance, an online exercise or activity.
- Spot the mistake or spot the difference exercise looking at visual or written documents.
- Examination of some equipment or artefacts with questions to answer.
- Multiple choice exercises.
- 'Write the question' activity. Learners are given a list of 10 key words. Their task is to devise five questions with correct answers to ask another group.
- Assembly line – learners are given a model to re-create or reassemble.

Subject specialist examples

- *Accounting*
  Activity 1 Crossword – accounting definitions.
  Activity 2 Experiment table – what happens if sales were changed on the cash flow?
  Activity 3 Business documents or accounts with deliberate errors which need correcting.
  Activity 4 Gapped handout with key words missing.

- *Plumbing*
  Activity 1 Mix and match cards: health and safety symbols and definitions.
  Activity 2 Experiment table – what happens if …?
  Activity 3 Two test questions to answer with text books to consult.
  Activity 4 'Name the components or parts' identification exercise.

Carousel 'learning stations' can also be useful where you want learners to experience or experiment with a range of products, equipment, techniques or skills within a lesson. For example:

- *Art and Design* – four stations set up for learners to experiment with four different printing techniques.
- *Catering* – four different 'tasting' stations for cheeses or fruits, for example.
- *Early Years* – four different types of 'messy' play to experience.
- *Science* – four different roles of systems in the human body.
- *Woodwork* – four different wood joints to compare and contrast.

18 Using Recipes

A concept, a procedure or an event may be more easily understood or explained if it is broken down into component parts.

The illustration below is an example of a blank recipe card which the teacher could modify to use with learners in many different ways. As well as aiding the recall and revision of key facts, the activity could encourage learners to make choices, decisions and help with planning and sequencing.

It could be used to introduce a topic to help you and the learners identify what they already know. They could then return to their recipes at the end of the topic and make additions or changes to their first ideas, based on their new learning.

What to do

1 To make the recipe card you can copy the illustration in Figure 18.1 or adapt the headings to suit your particular circumstances.
2 Provide each learner with a recipe card and ask them to compile a recipe which represents a given topic.
3 When they have each compiled a recipe, they could share their recipes with a partner or explain their proposed ingredients to the rest of the group.

Recipe for a successful ....

Ingredients

g / oz

g / oz

g / oz

g / oz

g / oz

plus

a dash of ......

a sprinkle of ....

lots of ....

Figure 18.1

Variations

- Introduce an element of competition in which learners have to present their recipes to a panel of judges – the Michelin Chefs. Prizes could be awarded for originality, most appropriate selection of ingredients and so on.

- Learners fill in the first three sections of a recipe and then exchange them with other learners who will each complete another section.
- Learners are asked to produce a full meal which includes recipes for starter, main course and dessert.
- Learners present to a panel of peers who will judge each of the ideas and award points or prizes or sponsorship deals for the most creative ideas.
- Provide learners with a list of 'ingredients' from which they have to produce a successful recipe using *only four* ingredients from those listed.
- Provide learners with some ingredients and ask them to complete the recipe with their own ideas.
- Use images or real objects to represent ingredients.
- Recipes could be prepared on transparencies by learners and presented to the group for sharing and discussion using a traditional overhead projector.

Subject specialist examples

- *Business Studies* – recipe for a successful business plan or marketing strategy.
- *Early Years* – recipe for a successful nursery provision for 0–5 years.
- *Hairdressing* – recipe for a satisfied client in the salon.
- *IT/Creative Media* – recipe for an effective web page.
- *Key Skills* – recipe for a successful presentation or interview.
- *Performing Arts* – recipe for a successful production.
- *Sports Studies* – learners could produce three different recipes which represent training programmes for three different clients.
- *Study Skills* – recipe for a successful assignment.
- *Travel and Tourism* – recipe for a successful escorted visit.

19 Censored!

 This fun activity is excellent for recapping or revising a topic or subject using the whole class. It provides good developmental opportunities for communication skills and familiarity with subject-specific vocabulary. It encourages higher order thinking, requiring learners to explain and contextualize rather than simply recall. It also provides an element of competition with penalties for wrong answers.

What to do

1 Prepare a set of cards containing key words for the topic.
2 For this game the tutor takes on the role of adjudicator.
3 Divide the class into two teams, A and B, and give each team a set of cards.
4 A member of team A takes the top card from their pile and has to describe the key word on that card without mentioning it by name. This key word is the 'CENSORED!' word. The learner has to secretly share their 'CENSORED!' word with the adjudicator.
5 Each person from team B has to write down on a mini whiteboard what they think the 'CENSORED!' word is.
6 Each member from team B then holds up their whiteboard and a point is awarded for each correct answer.
7 If at any point the player mentions the word they are describing, the adjudicator must shout 'CENSORED!' and play passes to the opposite team.
8 If the person from team A gives the wrong explanation, then everyone on the opposite team gets two points. If the person decides to pass the card to another member of their team to describe the 'CENSORED!' word, then each correct answer by the opposite team gets two points.
9 After each explanation, the teams change sides until everyone has had a turn. The team with the higher number of points wins.

Practical tips

- The tutor or a selected group member needs to keep the score, as it can get quite complicated!
- Mini whiteboards can be made by laminating sheets of paper or card.
- Provide a reward for the winning team.

Variations

- The role of the adjudicator could be passed to a chosen learner in the group.
- The exercise could be done in smaller groups if the class is large. Each person is given a 'CENSORED!' card which they explain to the rest of the group. The first one to write down the key word on their mini whiteboard gets the point. If the person does not know the definition, then another person can offer to give an explanation to the group and gain two points. If this is wrong, two points will be lost.
- Visual images could be used rather than key words.
- This could be played in pairs. A board game format could be used, the person only moving forward on the roll of the die if the 'CENSORED!' word is correctly described.
- Ask learners to record the descriptions of the key words used as a revision exercise and research the words that were incorrectly described.

Subject specialist examples

- *Accountancy* – key words from a set of financial accounts.
- *English* – works by particular authors.
- *Health and Social Care* – key words from parts of the body.
- *Science* – key terminology across all topics, for example, digestion and respiration.

20 I'm in Charge

 This activity is primarily designed to be used where learners are participating in simulated work-based situations. It incorporates two effective teaching and learning strategies: peer teaching and peer assessment. Peer teaching can be particularly effective for diffident learners who may be reluctant to seek help from the tutor.

Further benefits offered by this activity include explaining to others, which is a helpful reinforcement technique while at the same time wider key skill development can be encouraged.

The tutor is required to undertake a watching brief throughout but if at all possible to assume a low profile.

What to do

1 The tutor allocates a particular management or supervisory role to one or several learners, for example, salon manager in a hair and beauty practical session.
2 Other learners will be engaged in the typical activities and procedures associated with that working environment, for example, reception duties, shampooing hair and so on.
3 The managers or supervisors assume responsibility for organizing and managing appropriate aspects of the session.
4 At the end of the session, the designated manager or supervisor is responsible for conducting a question and answer session or managing peer assessment of tasks.

Practical tips

- The managers or supervisors are given an appropriate badge or recognizable sign of office.
- Certain roles will require managers or supervisors with more expertise.

! Danger points

- The tutor must ensure learner understanding of the role. This is best done as a tutorial session before the session, possibly accompanied by a written 'job specification' which emphasizes the main learning points to be reinforced.
- Relevant health and safety issues must be closely monitored by the tutor.

Variations

- Allocate 'experts' whose responsibility is providing coaching as appropriate.
- A 'secret shopper' can be randomly chosen, the learner being 'sworn to secrecy' until the end of the session when they provide feedback on particular aspects requested by the tutor. For example, a 'secret shopper' could be asked to comment on customer service in a retail environment.

Subject specialist examples

- *Art and Design* – a learner could be allocated the role of resources manager, for instance, overseeing the distribution and return of materials.
- *Built Environment* – a site foreman can be responsible for checking the concrete mix or accuracy of measurements and so on.
- *Business Administration* – learners can be allocated relevant roles in a simulated office.
- *Catering* – an environmental health officer can be responsible for noting hygiene practices in food preparation and service.
- *ICT* – if learners use a workbook approach to learning, one student can be designated the role of 'spreadsheet expert', another can be the 'hyperlink expert'. The experts help students with difficulties in their designated areas.
- *Travel and Tourism* – undertaking a managerial role within a college-based travel agency.

Thinking points

Think about the domains of learning (affective, cognitive and psychomotor) and the stages of learning within those domains. How might these be applied in order to promote differentiated learning opportunities for individuals?

21 Speed Networking

This activity is based on the principles of speed dating! It is a very good way for all learners to have a short period of contact with everyone in the class, and if not the whole class, a very large group. It can be used as an icebreaker exercise, to gather and share ideas and information or for peers to offer feedback to one another.

What to do

1 Arrange a line of tables with chairs facing across the tables. For larger groups you may need two sets of tables and chairs.
2 Place a 'time out chair' at the end or head of the table (see Figure 21.1). This is essential for the exercise to succeed and for learners to network with each person.

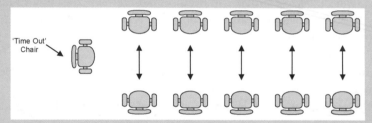

Figure 21.1

3 Ask learners to take a seat. One person needs to be seated in the odd chair at the table end. If you have an even number of learners, you will have to participate.
4 Before starting, explain the 'rules of engagement' – in other words, what information is to be exchanged? Are the learners required to take notes?
5 Signal the start. Learners will talk across the table to the partner facing them.
6 After 3 or 4 minutes, signal to stop and ask that each learner moves to their left. They will now be seated opposite a new partner.
7 Sign the start and repeat until the learners have returned to their original partner.
8 A different learner will move into the 'time out chair' each time. Since this person will not have a designated partner at this point, they can either observe or take 'time out' to review their notes.

Practical tips

- Have some method of gaining attention to signal the time to move on, for example, a bell, whistle or buzzer.
- Learners may need frequent reminders of the direction in which they should move.

- If learners are recording information, they may need 'something to rest on' while they write.
- The activity requires careful consideration of seating and furniture so ensure enough time is allowed for this either before or during a lesson.

! Danger points

- Brief learners about safe handling and movement of furniture during the setting-up stage. For example, chair legs waving in the air at eye level can be a particular hazard!
- Some learners, particularly those with literacy difficulties, may find it difficult to record information in a short period of time.

Variations

- Use as an icebreaker, for example, learners exchange names and ask typical icebreaker questions.

22 Organizing an Event

This approach provides opportunities for learners to research a topic and show off their learning in a creative way. They will be asked to take on responsibility for the organization and management of an occasion as well as learning about a particular area of a subject.

Handing over an event to learners to organise can present them with a wide range of opportunities for learning and personal development.

As well as exploring an area relating to a particular topic, it is also a chance to integrate and practise a range of key and transferable skills.

It will encourage learners to work collaboratively, manage their time and work to deadlines.

What to do

1   Decide on the focus for the event. The topic could be an area you select from the syllabus which would be appropriate for this approach or you could decide upon an area of interest through discussion with your learners.
2   Depending on the scale of the project you will need to ensure you have allowed enough time for the necessary planning and organization.
3   You should try to work *with* the learners but aim to give them as much freedom and responsibility as possible.

The following is an example of an event which a group of learners might organise:

A group of learners on a Health and Social Care course take on the planning and organization of a Culture Day as part of a module looking at Culture and Diversity. The event is to take place in a college and the learners should be encouraged to take on the organization and management of the day themselves, with only minimal involvement from teaching staff.

The learners organise themselves into subgroups and each choose a different culture to research. Each subgroup assumes responsibility for preparing and 'hosting' a stand which would showcase their chosen culture. They are free to decide how they would like to present their ideas.

As well as exploring their chosen culture, the learners will also need to make all the necessary practical arrangements for the event, including bookings for a suitable venue and equipment, publicity, invitations, liaison with key personnel in the college and organization on the day.

The activity demands a great deal of the learners and places responsibility on them which some may not have experienced before. It can also be extremely valuable in building confidence and discovering hidden talents in the learners!

Practical tips

- The more freedom the learners have in planning, organizing and sometimes learning from mistakes, the better. However, the tutor does need to keep a 'watching brief' as they will still have the usual professional responsibilities.

Variations

- Set up a wiki for the learners to develop their ideas on and to produce their shared materials. A wiki is a useful web-based communication tool to facilitate group work and will also enable your learners to experience another aspect of ICT. Wikis are a way for groups to access a web page and create a shared document which they can then read and edit. It helps to keep all the planning, changes and shared ideas for a group project in one place and because it is online, learners can access it at a time and place to suit them.
- It might provide an opportunity for learners from different curriculum areas to work together to combine their ideas and expertise in arranging a joint venture. For example, learners from a Health and Social Care course could work with a group from an Art and Design programme.
- Increasingly, institutions are looking at the educational possibilities of using virtual worlds such as Second Life® with their learners. Second Life® is a 3-D virtual world and provides users with the facility to build 3-D virtual communities. Teachers who have institutional access to this type of resource might want to explore the possibility of creating a 'virtual event' with their learners.

Subject specialist examples

- *Catering* – learners organise an end-of-year event for local employers.
- *Early Years* – students who are approaching the end of their course could organise an Open Evening for prospective learners. Staff from placement providers such as nursery managers could also be invited. It could be an opportunity to invite young people from local schools who might then be encouraged to apply to a college at some time in the future.
- *Health and Social Care* – learners could organise a 'Diversity' event. Learners could produce ethnic dishes for tasting, wear national costumes and so on.
- *Performing Arts* – learners organise a trip to the theatre for a specified group to include a tour and associated workshops showcasing particular aspects of theatre and performing arts. An important feature of this would be that learners would need to make contact and liaise closely with staff at the local theatre.
- *Sports Studies* – organise an event to show the different options for including exercise in daily lifestyles. Learners could invite staff and students from their college or extend the invitation more widely to include local schools or other organizations.

- *Technology* – learners organise a Technology Fair within their college. They could use the event to showcase new and innovative ideas which they have created while on the course. Invitations could be extended to local employers and university departments.

What next?

- For more information about 3-D virtual worlds, access the Second Life® website at http://secondlife.com.
- To find out more about using wikis, access http://www.wikispaces.com.
- A helpful resource about the use of wikis in learning and teaching can be found at: http://www.sddu.leeds.ac.uk/online_resources/wikis/index.php.
- If you are interested in setting up a wiki, a useful starting place is http://pbwiki.com where you will also find an area focusing specifically on using wikis in teaching and learning: http://pbwiki. com/education.wiki.

23 Rainbow Groups

 Peer teaching can be used to provide a student-centred approach and this technique aims to engage all learners from the start of a lesson, encouraging them to develop their research skills and communication skills as well. Rainbow groups are an effective way to get different students working together and to get everyone involved.

Learners are provided with templates to complete and these can be very helpful to students as it gives a uniform framework for all learners to record their ideas and work in progress. Use of a common template also assists the learners in how to contrast and compare information they have gathered.

What to do

1   Before the lesson, break the new subject down into sub-topics. For example, in Business Studies, the topic 'Types of Organization' could be divided into four sub-topics: sole traders, partnerships, limited companies and non-profit-making organizations.
2   Prepare a differently coloured set of cards for each sub-topic.
3   Prepare case study materials, handouts, internet printouts and so on relating to the different sub-topics.
4   Prepare a blank template grid (see Figure 23.1 for one completed for Business Studies). Each learner will need a copy of the template grid.
5   Divide the learners into groups, based on the number of sub-topics. The number of learners in each group must be the same or greater than the number of sub-topics.
6   Each learner receives a coloured card and forms a table group with others of that colour, for example, all learners with red cards sit together.
7   Provide a selection of appropriate research materials for each table group.
8   Using the research materials provided the learners will work together to explore their sub-topic. Each learner will then complete relevant sections of their personal template grid.
9   The groups are reconstituted into 'Rainbow Groups'. Within these new groups, all colours (sub-topics) must be represented. Using the information on their grid, each learner takes it in turn to teach their sub-topic to others in the group.
10   At the end of the activity, each learner should have a completed template.
11   The teacher conducts a review with the whole group to reinforce and supplement any information as appropriate.

Practical tips

*   Careful selection of sub-topics, research material and group composition affords many opportunities for differentiation within this activity, for example, a selected group could be allocated a more complex topic.

! Danger points

- For the activity to run successfully, remember that the number of learners in each group must be the same as or greater than the number of sub-topics.

Variations

- Learners find the research materials themselves before they start completing the template.
- As a feedback exercise, learners from each colour group explain and fill in a large 'master' blank template at the front of the room with guidance from the teacher and the other group members.
- Learners devise a quiz on their own sub-topic to test other groups.

Subject specialist examples

- *Art and Design* – comparing artists from a particular school.
- *Business Studies* – Types of organization grid template (Figure 23.1).

Type of organization	No. of owners	Characteristics of this organization	Advantages	Disadvantages	How are profits shared?	Liability?
Sole trader						
Partnerships						
Limited Companies						
Non-profit making organization						

Figure 23.1

- *Health and Social Care* – find out about a range of different care providers.
- *Media* – comparing and contrasting genre.
- *Science* – properties and reactivity of groups of elements from the Periodic Table.

24 Just a Minute

This is a noisy, fun exercise for the end of a session or for a revision activity at the end of a topic. It is based on a long-running radio programme. This activity is useful for developing communication skills and confidence in public speaking.

What to do

1 Collect some props for the activity including items such as humorous hooters, whistles and a stopwatch.
2 Prepare a series of cards with a subject word or sentence written on them.
3 Appoint a person from the group to be timekeeper and scorer. The person selected does not take part in the game. The tutor acts as chairperson.
4 Divide the class into two teams.
5 Cards are issued to members of the team in turn. The learner then attempts to talk on the subject for a specified period of time. If he or she is successful, they gain a point.
6 Inaccuracies and hesitation can be challenged by the opposite team who will blow their whistles or honk their horns.
7 If the chairperson considers the challenge reasonable, then bonus points are awarded and the topic passes to the challengers who must take over the topic and continue talking until the minute is up.
8 Whoever is speaking at the end of the minute is awarded a point.

Practical tips

- Produce a mix of topics to encompass subject specifics, generic study skills and assignment-related points, and so on.
- Include a few 'joker' cards for fun.
- Mark the backs of the cards in some way so that the mix can be manipulated to facilitate inclusion.
- The detail on the card acts as a catalyst for sharing information. The tutor is able to reflect on what knowledge is *not* coming to the fore and may need to adjust future revision accordingly.

! Danger points

- Learners may be anxious about interrupting and taking over the subject so the chairperson needs to award random bonus points freely.

Variations

- Have an 'all or nothing approach' when no interruptions are allowed from the other team and points only awarded on completion of the allocated time.
- Team members can decide among themselves who will talk on the allocated subject.
- As part of an end-of-module exercise, learners could be asked to provide suitable topics and prepare a series of cards. These cards could then be 'road tested' to ensure there is sufficient material to develop. A basic resource bank could be initiated to be supplemented by tutors.

Subject specialist examples

Possible topics to speak about include:

- *Art* – Post-Impressionists, acrylics as a medium, throwing a pot.
- *Built Environment* – protective apparel, implementing a three-phase wiring system.
- *Business Studies* – the marketing mix, book-keeping, international trading.
- *Entry to Employment* – responding to an advertisement, preparing for an interview, job search skills.
- *Holistic Therapies* – aromatherapy oils, Reiki massage, removal of unwanted facial hair.
- *Law* – mens rea, tort, a common assault, the Crown Court.
- *Social Sciences* – Jungian psychology, the class system, the penal system.
- *Travel and Tourism* – ethical resort development, emergency evacuation procedures, the National Trust.

25 Film Festival

There are many films, documentaries and TV programmes which have links or are of direct relevance to specialist subjects and curriculum areas. A selection could be researched, collected and shown to learners as an event or 'Film Festival'.

What to do

1 Research and collect a range of relevant material. This could be a varied selection of well-known 'blockbuster' films, classic films, documentaries and TV programmes. Your theme for the event could be broad-ranging or more specific.
2 Set aside a whole day or part day for the festival and plan a viewing schedule with a choice of programme. The size of the event and number of learners attending will determine the number of rooms and AV facilities required.
3 Make a programme and plan publicity and advertising within the organization to raise the profile and build expectation. Planning will need to allow time for movement between rooms, breaks and review periods.
4 Where appropriate, provide the learners with a synopsis of the films giving advance information.
5 Devise handouts or worksheets for learners to complete for reviewing and making connections to their own learning.

! Danger points

- Check your organization's copyright agreements and seek advice.
- Be aware of the certification of the films to be shown and suitability for the learners.
- Recognize cultural sensitivities which may exist within the group.
- Learners may need to be provided with an 'opt out' or alternative choice having considered the synopsis.

Variations

- Learners could take responsibility for some or all of the festival, for example, elements of the planning.
- Consider simple refreshments.

- Build in features to make the event a 'red carpet' event. For example, a photographer and roving reporter with a video camera asking for reactions and thoughts. It may be possible to involve learners from other departments, for example, media learners could provide a 'news item' regarding the event for circulation on the college intranet.
- A plenary could be held at the end of the event with planned questions for discussion.
- Learners could make short films on researched, allocated topics. These films then become the focus of a film festival at a future date.
- Learners could film a practical demonstration to show others in the group, for example, in science, an experiment showing chemical reactions.

What next?

The British Film Institute (BFI) website includes an Education Zone which offers advice and material online to download for free: http://www.screenonline.org.uk/education. The site includes access to moving image material categorized and searchable by subject area together with teaching packs and guides. The BFI online guide *Moving Images in the Classroom* offers advice and techniques for integrating film and television into the curriculum.

The British Board of Film Classification, the independent regulator of the film and video industry in the UK, provides guidance and information on classification categories. Their website is: www.bbfc.co.uk.

26 Explain to the Aliens

 It is important to establish firm foundations in order to build and scaffold new or more advanced learning. As teachers, we often take for granted or, in some cases, underestimate what learners already know and understand. This can then lead to new learning being pitched inappropriately.

This activity can be helpful as an assessment of learning. As well as providing opportunities for learners to revisit topics, it also helps them practise useful skills including the use of an index, skimming and scanning of texts, sorting and prioritising information, working collaboratively, presenting and communicating ideas.

The activity could be used before a new topic is introduced to check learners' understanding, to recall prior learning and to identify gaps or misunderstanding. Alternatively, the activity can be used towards the end of a topic or key phase in a lesson, in order to review and consolidate new learning.

Learners are likely to learn through the process of researching their given topic. They are also likely to learn through their peers; discussing and sharing in their subgroups and through peer learning in the final presentations.

What to do

1   Divide the group into smaller subgroups, ideally 4–5 learners per group.
2   Each group is then given a specific topic or question to research which relates to the general topic for the lesson. Learners will need to research relevant information and then prepare a presentation to explain their ideas clearly to a group of 'aliens'.
3   You (the teacher?) should emphasize the importance of providing clear and precise explanations as the 'aliens' they will be assisting may not be familiar with specialist vocabulary, processes and terminology.
4   Each group should have access to a range of relevant materials which they can use for their research. These may include books, journals and web-based materials.
5   Set a time limit for groups to research their topic and a further time limit to prepare their presentations.
6   You might want to suggest that each student has a particular role or area of responsibility within their group such as a timekeeper, a manager to ensure everyone is involved and a scribe to record information.
7   After a set time, each subgroup then has to explain their allocated topic or question to the rest of the group – who take on the role of the 'aliens'. They are aiming to explain so that the 'aliens' all understand what they have been 'taught'. At this stage the 'aliens' are not allowed to ask any questions or seek clarification.
8   The 'aliens' will then be given a short test to check their understanding. The test could be written, verbal or require the aliens to demonstrate a skill.

Variations

- Learners work individually and present their ideas to a small group. This could be helpful for learners who may feel daunted by presenting to larger groups.
- The 'aliens' are each allowed to ask *one* question to seek clarification or gather further information.
- The presentation could be in a visual format using a maximum of 10 words to support it.
- Each group is given specific sources which they have to use to gather their information. These could be set texts, library books, learners' own notes. This could be helpful where learners are normally reluctant to use these sources and need to be reminded of their importance and value.

Subject specialist examples

- *Biology* – chemical reactions associated with photosynthesis.
- *Built Environment* – the different bonding patterns used in bricklaying.
- *Early Years* – common childhood illnesses.
- *English* or *Communications* – different parts of speech.
- *Law* – different claims in employment law.
- *Science* – impact of global warming.
- *Sport Science* – structure and function of main muscle groups.

This approach could also be used to explain how to perform a particular practical skill or process. Learners should be asked to both describe and explain each stage to encourage them to show their understanding of the process as well as each step involved.

- *Catering* – silver service.
- *Hairdressing* – applying colours.
- *Health and Social Care* – bathing an elderly client in a care home.

What next?

If you are interested in using peer learning and assessment, the link below provides some further information and materials about the varieties, benefits and problems associated with these techniques: http://www.leeds.ac.uk/sddu/lt/teachtalk/n_falchikov.htm.

Information Literacy – The University of Huddersfield has developed an interactive guide to research techniques and strategies. It is designed to support the development of the skills required to find information in libraries and online: http://www.hud.ac.uk/cls/infolit/.

27 E-Treasure Hunt

 Learners are increasingly likely to be familiar with the internet as a source of information. For some, however, the web can be a confusing and distracting place.

Some learners may not use it effectively and will benefit from supported activities which are designed to help them navigate the web and use it as a tool for research and learning. This activity helps learners to develop the necessary skills to navigate websites effectively and is particularly useful when introducing a new topic.

What to do

1 Book a computer room.
2 Organize the learners individually or in pairs at each computer.
3 Provide the learners with a list of questions, images or facts you want them to find out from the internet.
4 Provide a list of websites which the learners will be expected to use to retrieve the required answers and information.
5 Structure the task to include a greater degree of challenge as learners' skills in finding and retrieving information develop.
6 Set a time limit for the learners to find the information.
7 Allow time for group feedback during which learners can mark and discuss their findings.
8 Offer a prize for the most correct answers.

Practical tips

- At the start it is advisable to limit the research to the websites provided. As the learners become more proficient and confident, they can be encouraged to explore websites more widely.
- In preparing the treasure hunt, try to ensure that some of the information is easy to locate on the web page, with other answers requiring more skilled navigation as the learner becomes more confident.
- Encourage the more able learners to show the less skilled ones how to find the information they have missed.

! Danger points

- Test the E-Treasure Hunt first, as website data can change regularly.
- Constantly check learners are not mis-using the internet for their own private use.

- When learners are designing their own E-Treasure Hunts, help them to ensure that the data for their topic are from reliable sources. Encourage them to evaluate the quality of different website information.

Variations

- Ask learners to design their own E-Treasure Hunt for different topics and then ask them to exchange their questions with others in the group.
- Give each learner a different image to find on the internet and then ask them to bring all their information together to discover the theme of the topic.
- If internet access is not possible, this activity could be adapted to use with textbooks, newspapers and journals instead.
- Further research on topics could be carried out using other resources, such as textbooks, newspapers and journals. These different resources could be evaluated in terms of their currency, validity and reliability.

Subject specialist examples

- *Accountancy* – deduce key words from given descriptions of terms, such as fixed assets, debtors and debentures.
- *Business Studies* – find information about the marketing strategies of different businesses.
- *Performing Arts* – provide a group of photo images of different actors or playwrights, and ask learners to find out facts about them.
- *Travel and Tourism* – ask the learners to find a place or city from images or key facts given. This could be done as a competition between different groups.

What next?

The BECTA website at http://www.becta.org.uk is a useful starting point to explore the use of technology within education. The site provides a comprehensive guide to the latest innovations and applications of technology in an educational context.

Use of educational technology is a rich source of research study. One such paper which considers the use and effectiveness of web quests with undergraduates is:

Hassanien, A. (2006) An evaluation of the web quest as a computer based learning tool, *Research in Post-Compulsory Education*, 11(2): 235–50.

28 Jigsaws

When introducing a new topic, it is important to provide learners with an overview and to put the subject in context. Otherwise learners may progress through a series of unrelated chunks which they do not connect with prior knowledge or learning. Representing the topic as a jigsaw may assist some learners to see the whole picture; they can recognise where new knowledge and skills 'fit'.

What to do

1   Prepare a jigsaw template (either from computer sources or draw your own). Each piece should contain a subsection or a key word of a topic to be studied.
2   Provide each learner with a copy of the template to keep in their files and ask them to shade in each section as work is completed. This enables learners to see how far they have progressed and it also serves as a visual reminder of the whole topic.

Practical tips

- Use different colours for each jigsaw to make sorting easier.
- The simpler the shapes, the easier they are for cutting.
- Laminate card to make the pieces durable.
- Between four and 10 pieces per jigsaw is most manageable

! Danger points

- Use a large template and provide appropriate pens if learners are adding information to the jigsaw.

Variations

- Use photographs of a skill sequence which when pieced together make a linear jigsaw.
- Use a circle shape, made up of segments with key facts on each segment. Include some spare segments with 'rogue' statements on them. Ask learners to make a complete circle with no spaces. They can then self-check their knowledge either singly or in groups against a model answer.

- Divide a class for group work by preparing a series of simple jigsaws with four or five pieces. Use an image, for example, types of protective clothing cut into pieces or a simple statement. Ensure that each piece has the title of the subject on the back for easy sorting. Issue each learner with a piece of jigsaw and ask them to match pieces with other learners to make a group. They then work in that group for a period of time or an activity.
- Produce a wall of learning by marking off a section of display board and enlarging the jigsaw template to poster size. Ask learners to identify key points within each subsection and write their ideas in the relevant shape. This will provide an attractive display. Learners can photograph the poster and retain a copy for revision.
- Learners can develop ICT skills by producing a jigsaw collage of photographs which can be used as a background for mounting further display work.

Subject specialist examples

- *Art and Design* – learners are given a blank jigsaw template and a subject. Each learner then produces a statement or an image for each piece of the jigsaw thus building a visual representation of links within the topic.
- *Health and Social Care* – all learners are given a piece of a jigsaw containing only one key word or phrase of a master template, for example, services available to the housebound. Each learner researches the phrase on their piece and reports back to the group. The group is given a copy of the master template and adds information presented by other members.
- *SLDD* – learners can use a linear jigsaw to reinforce personal hygiene.

What next?

Accelerated Learning is a broad term relating to practical approaches to teaching. It suggests that a positive learning environment, combining auditory, visual and kinaesthetic approaches can motivate learners to greater achievement. If you are interested in finding out more about Accelerated Learning, investigate Alistair Smith's website at http://www.alite.co.uk.

29 Problem Page

This activity, inspired by 'Agony Aunt' and 'Problem Pages' in newspapers and magazines, can be adapted for many different courses at varying levels. The idea behind the activity is that learners consider problems or difficulties associated with their subject area generally. Alternatively, a particular area or scenario requiring a solution may be used. The learners, individually or in pairs, take the part of the 'Agony Aunt'.

Distancing a subject through the use of a third party, in this case the 'Agony Aunt', allows sensitive subjects to be explored more objectively or from a different perspective. Introducing the concept of problem solving with learners can develop higher order skills including critical thinking.

What to do

1   Identify four to six problems associated with a topic.
2   Describe these problems in the form of a short letter seeking advice (see Figure 29.1).

Figure 29.1

3   Transfer each of these problems to a separate text box, auto shape or table cell. Allow a space below each problem in which learners can write in their suggested solutions and advice.
4   Ask learners in pairs or groups of three to consider and discuss the problems and offer advice.
5   Consider each problem and ask a different group each time for their response, checking with other groups if they would like to suggest any different ideas.

Variations

- The title of the activity can be changed to suit the nature of a course. For example, learners on IT courses could be staffing a 'Help Desk'. Learners on a Leisure and Tourism course could be staffing a 'Tourist Information Office'.
- Learners could be given the problem page to research and complete for homework.
- Learners could be asked to identify and suggest the 'problems' and also model answers.
- Learners could offer advice to aid revision and study in theoretical subject areas.

Subject specialist examples

- *Art and Design* – care of materials and use of equipment. How to get the best results with certain techniques.
- *Business Studies* – ask for options as to how to raise finance for a business such as obtaining a new fleet of cars for a sales team.
- *Early Years* – common problems and questions often posed by parents such as how to introduce solid foods or successful toilet training.
- *Health and Beauty* – how to deal with common problems, for example, an itchy scalp, split ends.
- *Health and Social Care* – developing an activity programme for residents in a care home.
- *Hospitality and Catering* – how to remedy or prevent mishaps and how to deal with dissatisfied customers.
- *ICT* – how to manage file storage and retrieval.
- *Media* – in addition to writing the 'Problem Page', learners could use research techniques to study and analyse representation in different newspapers.

30 Using Puppets

 Puppets can be a fun and effective way to trigger communication and interaction, especially when dealing with sensitive or emotive subjects. The puppet can become a third party or medium which can offer learners a degree of anonymity or detachment. Although initially this approach may be considered more appropriate for young children, it is surprising how enthusiastic older learners become once they overcome any initial scepticism! In effect, the puppets become an extension of a more traditional role play activity. This approach enables the learner to take a less explicit part in a scenario while at the same time exploring or demonstrating their understanding of particular learning points.

What to do

1 Provide a selection of puppets for learners to use.
2 Simple finger puppets are cheap and effective.
3 You (or the learners) can also create your own puppets out of paper plates and sticks or socks with felt for the features.
4 Learners use their chosen puppet characters to act out given scenarios. Some learners might prefer to prepare a script for their puppet, others will be happy to be more spontaneous.

Practical tips

- Some learners might appreciate some rehearsal time.
- Often it is better to work in pairs or small groups rather than showcasing the puppets in action with a large group of learners.
- Provide props which learners can incorporate into their puppet scenarios.
- Assume that learners are likely to need a period of 'play time' to get used to their puppets, allow them to start thinking creatively and to experiment with puppets as a communication medium. In some cases, this time also helps some learners to overcome any initial self-consciousness.

Variations

- The puppet interactions can be recorded on video. This approach is especially helpful for 'camera-shy' learners because the learner takes on a 'back stage' role and it is the puppet which appears 'on screen'. They are able to present their ideas using the technology without themselves appearing on screen

Subject specialist examples

- *Early Years* – the learners provide the 'voice-over' to introduce their puppet characters, each of which represent different behaviour responses in children. The 'voice-over' would be a commentary as to suitable strategies an Early Years practitioner might use when caring for a young child displaying this type of behaviour. The puppet character would then in turn give a response.
- *Early Years* – the learners provide the 'voice-over' to show their puppets demonstrating speech development in babies and young children.
- *Health and Social Care* – puppets can be created and used to explore issues to do with stereotyping and diversity.
- *Psychology* – the learners act out a scenario where the puppets assume particular personalities or behavioural characteristics.
- *Teacher Education* – the learners act out a conversation between a trainee teacher and their mentor. The character of the selected puppets could be used to show the different types of relationship between mentors and their mentee.

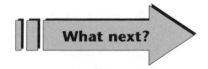

What next?

http://www.puppetsproject.com/ is a website with useful ideas and information about using puppets in the teaching of science.

31 Learning Landscapes

 This takes the principle of mind mapping and 'goes large'!

Learners with low levels of literacy and those who have difficulties expressing their understanding through linear text may find visual tools helpful. Notes and ideas can be captured and recorded using visual and spatial techniques. The principles of such tools are based on graphic visual displays which are not sequenced in a traditional linear form and which depict a subject using key words, images, symbols and colour. Mind maps can be described as such a tool and the technique is also known by other terms such as model maps, learning maps, cognitive maps, brain maps, webbing maps and spider grams.

It is suggested that the benefits of such visual tools are that they allow a visual overview and rapid appraisal of a large subject or topic area; they can represent a whole picture and detail simultaneously; they allow thoughts and random ideas to flow freely; they are attractive and therefore gain and hold attention; they encourage a subject to be viewed as an interconnected structure rather than a list of headings and subheadings; they use a minimal amount of words and postpone the need to sequence ideas and connect them.

What to do

1 Place a central key word or image on a blank page.
2 From this, main themes related to the central key word radiate out in the form of branches.
3 Each branch may divide into sub-branches.
4 Use images and symbols to represent words where possible.
5 Use colour to define and separate branches.

Creating a learning landscape

The idea is to create a growing map over a series of topic-related lessons, adding more and more information and extending over a larger and larger wall space. Use sheets of flip chart paper stuck together with tape to form a large paper covering for a blank wall. The reverse side of a roll of wallpaper or a paper tablecloth could also be used.

Create and add to the map by reviewing learning at key stages during a lesson, or at the end of a lesson. This may or may not be teacher-directed at the start as key branches are formed. Students can take responsibility for suggesting and creating sub-branches, words, images and photographs. After a few lessons, the wall display will be a collaboratively formed map of student learning, in fact the landscape of their learning. The learning landscape could be formed for many different subject areas and levels.

! Danger points

- Ideally, the learning landscape should be built up and displayed over a period of time. However, this may be problematic if the sessions are not taught in a base room, classroom space is shared or examinations are taking place. Remember to check these practical considerations in advance.

Variations

- A large landscape could be created in one lesson as a review activity. Divide a class into groups of three or four and give each group a sheet of flip chart paper and a key word heading. After each group has created a mind map using their key word, these can all be pinned to a large wall together to form a large mind map of the whole lesson.
- Students could be asked to research relevant websites to add useful detail for revision the following week. Higher level courses could research and add titles of relevant academic journal articles.
- Pin a roll of wallpaper (use lining paper or the reverse of a patterned roll) to run all the way around a room like a ribbon. At evenly spaced intervals, write or stick a pre-prepared key word/subheading from the lesson or topic. Allocate small groups to an area and ask them to develop the key word using mind map principles. After 5 minutes, ask each group to move to the left to read another group's key word and map. Continue in a carousel until each group has moved all the way round the room. This activity could be developed further by allowing groups to add further detail or information to each map section.
- A group could be asked to chart their 'learning journey' on a course to form an alternative form of landscape. Where were the metaphorical turning points, swamps, difficult stretches, bumpy paths, mountains to climb, easy roads?
- Use a digital camera to take pictures of the learning landscape in progress and the finished product. Learners could also be encouraged to capture their own record of images on their mobile phones. These images could then provide a useful visual revision aid or evidence of learning in a portfolio.

32 Memory Box

This is a useful activity for stimulating ideas and promoting creative thinking. It can be used at the start of a session to provide a focus for development. The activity may have particular appeal to visual and kinaesthetic learners.

What to do

1   Assemble a variety of related artefacts, photographs and fabrics and a series of 'memory box' containers. For example, a small plastic bucket could contain a sunhat, a bus or train ticket, a fabric bumble bee and so on. Between six and 10 objects is reasonable.
2   Share the topic of the session with the learners and ask them to select an item from the box and make some links with the topic.
3   Explore and expand the points made during the discussion.

Practical tips

- Charity shops and 'pound shops' are a useful source of artefacts.
- The memory box could consist of projected images if providing physical resources is difficult.

! Danger points

- The exercise loses its impact if the same objects are recycled too frequently.
- The items and containers will need to be classified in some way so a good filing system is necessary!

Variations

- Allocate a subject and ask each learner which five items they would include in a time capsule to represent that subject for future learners.
- Learners can be asked to assume the role of a given character and present a small oral living history presentation for the local media. This could provide a good basis for collaborative work within departments for an Open Day.

- Bags are placed on different tables around a classroom. Each bag contains a different task, activity, exercise, object, set of cards. Learners move round the room and bag activities in a carousel.

Subject specialist examples

- *English Language* – learners could use an old knapsack containing such items as a poppy, a recruiting poster and some old photographs for a session exploring war poetry.
- *Management* – learners could be asked to present on Human Needs theories, using items such as a piece of wallpaper, a friendship bracelet or a biscuit.
- *Performing Arts* – learners could select items and devise an improvisation on a theme.
- *Social Science* – could be asked to select items and provide a link with a political movement.

33 Learning Dice

 Using dice can introduce an element of chance and fun into lessons as the 'roll of the dice' can determine the path a learner must take. Playing with dice can increase motivation, interest and concentration while also offering the opportunity to develop learners' social and interpersonal skills. Dice games may be regarded as inclusive as all learners 'take a turn', they offer a tactile element for learners with kinaesthetic preferences and customised dice can be differentiated through content and design to meet the needs of individuals and groups.

- Numbers on standard dice can relate to specific numbered tasks which have to be completed.
- Numbers can be replaced with text, images or symbols.
- Textured dice can be used for learners with a visual impairment.
- Learners can design and make the dice themselves (see Figure 33.1).
- Different dice can be made for different stages in a lesson.

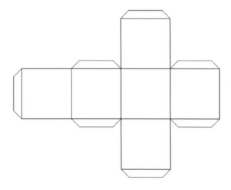

Figure 33.1

Starter dice

Make a die using a paper template or adapt existing dice. On each side of the die have one of the following:

- Devise three questions to ask about this topic.
- What do think will be hard about this topic?
- What do you think will be interesting about this topic?
- What do you think will be boring about this topic?
- Why will this topic be useful?
- What do you already know about this topic?

Review dice

- What was difficult about this topic?
- What are three questions to ask about this topic?
- What was the most interesting thing about this topic?
- Why was this topic relevant to the course?
- What do you understand really well about this topic?
- What other things would you like to know about this topic?

Generic dice

Label each side with a different word or phrase, for example, as shown in Figure 33.2.

Figure 33.2

Numeracy dice

Roll one die twice to get two numbers, then roll a second die labelled with mathematical equations (for example + or −) to be undertaken with the numbers.

People dice

Label sides of a die with representations of different groups (see Figure 33.3), for example, a family group; the elderly; two adults; one adult; one adult and one child; a child. Prepare a set of questions or scenarios which the learner must address with reference to the person or people on their roll of the die.

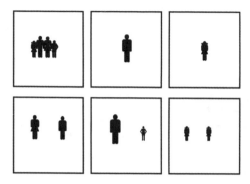

Figure 33.3

Language dice

Several dice are needed for this activity. Label the sides of the dice with differing parts of speech and punctuation, for example, noun, verb, adjective, exclamation mark and so on. Learners leave the dice in front of them and work towards producing a piece of writing which includes and identifies all the features identified on the dice.

First aid dice

Each face of the die states an occurrence appropriate for a first aid treatment. Learners suggest suitable interventions for that occurrence.

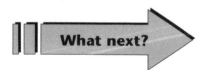

www.talkingdice.co.uk is a commercial website that offers a wide selection of picture dice for sale and also contains some downloadable ideas for using in lessons, particularly with ESOL learners.

34 Learning Ladders

 Using a ladder for learning can be helpful for visual and kinaesthetic learners. A ladder provides a visual aid which can help learners consider order, sequences and progression. Used in conjunction with flash cards or sticky notes, this resource allows learners to play around with their ideas before reaching a final decision.

What to do

1 Provide each learner or small group with an A4 laminated card depicting a suitable image of a ladder. You will find a selection of ladders on clipart or you could design your own. Ideally, there should be about 5–7 rungs on your ladder.

2 Prepare a set of cards with key words which are associated with a particular sequence. To make the task more challenging you can include some 'rogue' cards in the set.

3 Give each learner a set of sequence cards and ask them to arrange the cards on the ladder in the correct order (see Figure 34.1).

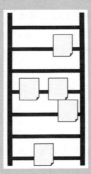

Figure 34.1

4 If the learners are working in small groups, ask them to discuss their ideas and justify their decisions as they work.

5 Give out a handout which covers all the key information – do they need to change anything?

Variations

- Learners are given blank sticky notes and have to add their own captions before placing them on the ladder.
- Learners are asked to place a sticky note on the ladder at the start of a lesson to indicate how much they know or how confident they feel about the topic they are about to explore in the

lesson. They can revisit their ladder at key points during the lesson and reposition their sticky note. This will help them to self-assess their learning while at the same time providing you with an opportunity to check on progress and learner confidence during the session

- Large copies of the ladder could be displayed in a classroom to provide a visual point of reference for sequences, order and associated key terms which learners need to become familiar with.

- To consolidate learning, learners are asked to devise a list of questions and answers of increasing difficulty about a particular topic. They then use their questions to test a partner or small group. The respondent scores a point on the ladder for each correct answer. The easiest question scores a point on the first rung and so on up the ladder. The aim is to climb the ladder to the top rung.

- Learners use a ladder to assess their own work or that of one of their peers. Having considered the work they place a marker which in their opinion represents their assessment and they then provide developmental feedback which suggests what might be done to improve the work in order to move the marker further up the ladder.

Subject specialist examples

- *Built Environment* – use a rope ladder and electrical or bulldog clips to provide learners with a more 'work-based' ambience, so encouraging them to make the link between their classroom and work-based learning.
- *Business Studies* – organise a business plan in chronological order.
- *Chemistry* – place a list of elements in ascending order of reactivity.
- *Early Years* – arrange an aspect of child development in chronological order.
- *First Aid* – place the steps for emergency resuscitation in order.
- *Health and Social Care* – arrange a care plan for a given client in order of priority.

 **What next?**

Geoff Petty has some ideas about self- and peer assessment which you might want to follow up at: http://www.geoffpetty.com/selfassess.html.

35 Roving Reporters

 Media and communications are an increasingly important part of many learners' everyday lives. Bringing in aspects of the media into teaching and learning can promote interest and variety and enable learners to draw on talents and skills that may otherwise be overlooked. The activity requires learners to interact with others, who may or may not be known to them. This can promote the development of self-confidence and the use and application of appropriate communication skills in a variety of contexts. They may also develop useful research skills and be challenged to summarise and present information using a variety of media.

What to do

1 In this activity, learners take on the role of reporters for a newspaper or television production.
2 Their brief is to go out and gather relevant information or research stories about a given topic from suitable venues or groups of people. Learners then use that information and research in further study which they can be asked to present in a variety of ways.

Examples

- Introduce a new topic by asking learners to go round and find out from other people in the college what they can tell them about that particular issue. The learners then present a short news article which summarises the findings.
- Conduct a 'vox pop' by asking learners and other people in the college their views on a particular topic.
- Arrange for learners to visit an 'expert' in the topic they are learning about and ask them to use the visit to conduct a short interview with that expert.

! Danger points

- Teachers will need to consider health and safety and supervision when learners are carrying out their research and coming into contact with individuals outside the classroom. This will be especially important when working with young people and vulnerable adults.
- Teachers will need to brief learners with regard to protocols and social conventions.
- Attention will need to be given to any relevant ethical points in relation to collecting, storing and publishing data.

Variations

- Use the technique to introduce research skills and data collection. The results can then be used to practise numeracy and IT skills by collating data and producing databases and graphs for statistical analysis.
- Learners produce a short video or audio recording which is then played back as a 'television' or 'radio' feature.
- Learners use their findings as the basis for the production of a newspaper article. Articles can then be compiled into a newspaper which represents a range of different articles and perspectives.

Subject specialist examples

- *Built Environment* – conduct a series of interviews with representatives from the local planning office, architect's office and building firms to elicit views on the use of alternative energy sources.
- *Business Studies* – arrange to meet with local employers to find out about the concerns of local businesses in the area.
- *English* – Chaucer and Shakespeare conduct a modern interview with historical characters.
- *Health and Social Care* – find out people's views about banning smoking in public places.
- *Media* – conduct interviews to gather views and opinions about film censorship and the extent to which films should be classified.
- *Psychology* – conduct an interview with main theorists (played by learners) to find out about their key ideas, asking them to explain and justify their research findings.
- *Sport and Leisure* – find out about the extent to which young people participate in sport and exercise. This could then be extended to find out about the scope of provision of exercise facilities for young people in the local area.
- *Teacher Education* – trainee teachers informally research learners' opinions about what makes an effective lesson.

36 In the Frame

 This activity helps learners to see the whole picture and 'frame' their learning. It can be used as a revision exercise which will generate display material for the learning space. It involves learners in research, thus building information-seeking skills. The size limitation of the frame can also encourage learners to be discriminating and succinct in their presentation of knowledge.

What to do

1 Mock up a series of large frames on the wall or whiteboard. These will become a blank canvas.
2 Each frame has a different sub-topic title. For example, if the general topic is 'Political Parties' each sub-topic frame will have a different focus, for instance, 'The Green Party'.
3 Learners work in small groups and are allocated a sub-topic to research.
4 Provide websites and other resources and indicate how much time is allowed for research.
5 Provide each group with a supply of postcard-size pieces of coloured paper or card and a supply of glue sticks.
6 Each group fills 'their' frame with fact cards.
7 At the end of the session the teacher recaps the points made by the frames in the gallery.
8 Learners can be encouraged to photograph the frames for future revision.

Practical tips

- Coloured adhesive tape can be used to make a frame. Alternatively learners can design a frame using ICT, which can be enlarged to poster size.
- Old picture frames, minus the glass, can also be used. Ornate frames can add an element of interest and can be held or supported on an easel.

! Danger points

- If students are using actual frames, remove all glass and smooth rough edges over with tape.
- Obtain permission to use student photographs.
- Consider asking the construction department to produce a type of easel which will obviate holding a frame for long periods.

Variations

- A learner can be allocated a historical persona and be photographed in an actual frame; the image then is used with text to make a mock newspaper article. Providing props can add interest and fun.
- A learning gallery can be built up as a frieze around the room over the duration of the topic.
- As part of the induction period, learners can work in pairs and introduce the person in the frame. A large group photograph can then be produced.
- Issue each learner with a sticky note on which to describe their current knowledge of the subject under consideration. Stick these notes on one frame and use as a baseline to work from. At the end of the session, ask the learners to identify their learning in the session on another sticky note which is placed in the second frame.

Subject specialist examples

- *Business* – each frame can represent responsibilities of personnel within an organization.
- *Hair and Beauty* – each frame can represent a face shape. Learners produce magazine illustrations or drawings to denote the most flattering shapes of hair style.
- *Health and Social Care* – learners produce a series of frames containing information under the title of 'Primary Health Care'.
- *Science* – learners work in groups to research a given character, for example, Crick or Darwin. One learner is 'in the frame', holding it to their face while the members of the group disseminate information about him or her.
- *Social Studies* – a group of learners are chosen to represent candidates in an election. The candidates are in the frame and deliver their address. At the end of the speeches the remainder of the learners cast their vote.

37 In the Mood for Music

 The effect of music on the moods, emotions, development and behaviour of both individuals and groups has been noted throughout history. Music can be used in many different ways to enhance teaching and promote learning.

At the beginning of lessons

Using background music can create a pleasant and inviting learning environment and can be part of a strategy to welcome learners to a class. It can help learners to feel at ease, reduce anxiety and break down barriers, particularly at the start of a course. Teachers who use music often comment that it helps them create a supportive and relaxed learning atmosphere. They deliberately use calming music to reduce learner tension and stress. The first session of any course is one of the single most important occasions and learners are often very quiet, silent even. Merely talking to another person can be an ordeal if everyone else can hear what is being said. If background music is playing before a class starts, learners may feel less anxious and maybe more likely to start a conversation and interact.

Learners have demonstrated that they are sensitive to the effect of music on the classroom environment and atmosphere, with many remarking that they have found the use of background music relaxing, soothing and calming.

Music as a classroom management tool

Music can be a classroom management tool, helping to create a receptive state for learning. Appropriate choices can energize, motivate, relax, calm, focus and link to a theme or a certain stage in the course. Music can be used as a timing device during group or individual tasks and exercises. For example, a 5-minute track can be selected to signify the length of a task. Music can be especially valuable at the start of a course when some learners can be self-conscious and hesitant about participating in group work. It can helpfully blend and mask those dominant and confident voices which may be off-putting to others. Some teachers also find that music can give some privacy when feeding back to individual learners or groups.

Music can signpost the start and finish particular sections of a lesson. When you are ready to begin a class, simply turning off the music can give a subtle auditory signal that the lesson is about to start. It can be used throughout break time with a different 'upbeat' track used towards the end to signify that the lesson will resume, for example, in 2 minutes' time. Active parts of a lesson, where students are required to move around to complete a task or to clear up, can be promoted with lively energetic music. Reflective, contemplative periods in a lesson can be enhanced by quiet music in the background. Music played at the end of a lesson can promote a positive feeling as students are leaving. Celebratory moments in a course can be recognised and made more enjoyable and memorable.

Themed music and 'soundtracks'

A backing soundtrack for a series of images, statistics or statements on PowerPoint or transparencies can replace verbal exposition and teacher talk – and have far greater impact! Themed soundtracks can be compiled to complement and enhance a subject or topic. For example, a piece of music could be selected from a film or TV programme which is linked to a topic. Connections may be made between a particular song title or group name and a specific module, unit, concept or skill.

Music to promote diversity and inclusion

Music from different cultures can be used to reach out to learners and can be a way of recognizing and valuing diversity. One student of West African origin felt he had been valued as an individual when a teacher researched and subsequently used West African music in a lesson.

Through the use of background drumming music in one lesson, a teacher found something in common with a learner where this had previously been difficult. Rap and hip hop have also been used to engage and motivate younger learners with low levels of literacy. In one project, hip hop lyrics were used to teach imagery, assonance, alliteration, rhythm and rhyme. Learners were then encouraged to write creatively in rap form using techniques they had learned.

Music to consolidate and reinforce

Learners may find raps and chants a useful tool for reinforcement and revision and may even enjoy composing and performing their own. A fun quiz where learners recognise popular theme tunes in 'hooked on classics' formats could be a first step in developing the confidence to transfer skills to word recognition. A sequence of differing and emotive musical mood pieces could be played in an exercise to develop the use of adjectives. Learners could be given some unfamiliar song lyrics and asked to guess whether, for instance, the music would be fast, slow, melancholy or jolly before listening to see if their impression matched the tunes.

! Danger points

- Many students do respond positively to background music in lessons, but sensitivity needs to be shown towards those who may dislike certain music or find it distracting or intrusive. Teachers should exert care, investigating and researching individual student needs and preferences. It is important to respect learning differences and to check that music does not distract or hinder learning, particularly during individual study time.
- Be aware and take advice on copyright issues if you are unsure of these.
- Take care with compilation albums – the first track may be ideal but if left playing might lead on to tracks which really do not really suit a lesson.

Thinking points

Consider a particular topic and research a piece of music which could link in some way. This could be through the lyrics, a connection to a period of time in history or 'era' or the name of the composer or group.

There can be strong links between music and personal identity. Response to different types of music can vary widely between individuals. How will you manage this?

What next?

Howard Gardner's much-debated Multiple Intelligence (MI) theory includes a 'Musical Intelligence': Gardner, H. (1983) *Frames of Mind: The Theory of Multiple Intelligence*. New York: Basic Books.

Jensen, E. (2000) *Music with the Brain in Mind*. San Diego: The Brain Store, Inc. This is an American perspective but may be of interest if you wish to read more about music and education.

The '*Mozart effect*' – the ability of Baroque-type music to improve intelligence and increase learning has been popularized. However, academic opinion is divided and the debate continues: McKelvie, P. and Low, J. (2002), Listening to Mozart does not improve children's spatial ability: Final curtains for the Mozart Effect, *British Journal of Developmental Psychology*, 20: 214–58.

38 Web Chat: Online Discussion Groups

Arguably the mention of technology and e-learning seems to elicit a more polarized response from teachers and learners alike than any other teaching and learning technique – even more so than role play! Typically, you either belong to the 'Luddite camp' or the 'best thing since sliced bread' brigade. The 'Luddites' can give you every excuse in the world for not bothering with technology – lack of skills, lack of technical support, cost and time being top of most lists, while the enthusiasts would argue that we all live in a technological age, people expect to use it, it excites, interests and motivates and it reaches people at a time and place which suit them.

Like any strategy in teaching and learning, technology and e-learning are tools which are available to teachers. Potentially, they open up possibilities which other techniques are unable to match but at the same time they have their limitations and problems.

Online discussion

The idea that learners and teachers discuss ideas and concepts is hardly revolutionary and indeed one might be hard pressed to observe a group of learners being taught where discussion in some shape or form does not take place. If one considers the constructivist principles of teaching and learning or learning as being a social activity, then discussion and exchange of ideas would be high on the list of relevant strategies to illustrate these theoretical concepts.

Web-based discussion is simply an extension of those principles but it has the potential for learners to meet and discuss without necessarily being in the same place at the same time.

Setting up any web-based discussion will require a degree of preparation and supervision, although the latter could potentially be shared with or designated to individual learners rather than the teacher.

In most instances, the discussion forum would be an area for sharing ideas relating to tasks or activities which learners have been given to work on. The forum would be the focal point for sharing and development of ideas arising from such activities.

It is often best to link the forum with the assessment process. Otherwise learners may be reluctant to get involved or view it as an optional extra, especially if they have not appreciated the possible benefits in using such activities.

What to do

1   If your institution has a Virtual Learning Environment, it is best to set up your discussion forum in that space.
2   Check that all your learners have access to the site and are aware of their user names and passwords if required.
3   Decide on the topic(s) or questions you want the learners to explore and give each of these a designated area within the forum.
4   Post a welcome note onto the main page with clear, concise instructions for the learners to

follow. It is important that your messages and instructions are easy to follow and un-ambiguous as you will not be around to clarify things!

5   Try to ensure the site is easy to find and does not involve too many stages to reach it – no more than three clicks if possible!!

6   When you introduce the learners to the site, consider having some 'practice/fun' time to get them used to the technology and get over any initial anxieties they may have. This is especially important if their activity on the forum is linked to the assessment process.

7   Consider providing an email contact where individuals can contact you if they are having difficulties with the technology or the activity itself.

8   If participants have not met face to face, it is often good to have an online icebreaker to enable individuals to start to gel as a group and to get to know something about each other.

9   Monitor the progress of the discussion and be prepared to step in to manage, motivate, challenge and encourage as appropriate.

10 Do not expect too much too soon. It can take some time for some people to get involved and just like a group of learners in a classroom it is likely that the group dynamic will experience ups and downs with peaks and troughs of activity.

! Danger points

Online discussion groups can have potential problems and limitations:

- As in a classroom setting some learners may have a lack self-confidence. In activities of this sort, it could be in their own skills to post messages – this could be related to the subject under discussion or their use of the technology. Learners may benefit from an induction into the discussion area to ensure they have the requisite essential skills to navigate to the site and are able to find their way around the area.
- Consider agreeing some 'ground rules' or 'netiquette' with the group before the forum is launched. This helps to raise learners' awareness as to the consequences of engaging in insensitive, inappropriate or unacceptable behaviour when online. This may help to avoid problems later which could arise where learners have not fully realized the nature of online communication.
- Difficulties with access to the discussion area, especially if the learner does not have internet access at home. Potentially, they could feel excluded from the group and the learning.
- Lack of focus – without someone managing the discussion, participants may wander off the point. This can be a positive aspect, giving learners the freedom to explore other issues of interest but as the facilitator you will need to agree the degree of freedom and flexibility which is appropriate for the group.
- Motivation – some learners may lose interest in the activity and once the initial novelty has worn off participation may decrease. It can be advisable to set a time limit for the discussion or stipulate a minimum number of postings for each learner.
- Time delay for a response – this type of technology sets up an expectation of a speedy response. If learners post a contribution and do not receive a prompt response they may lose interest or motivation or feel their contribution has not been valued.

- Needs regular 'pruning' – it can be off-putting if there are too many contributions to read. It helps if there is a framework set up for the discussion area which groups similar threads together under 'subheadings'.
- Nature of the contributions – some discussion areas offer the option for people to post anonymous contributions. While this may have advantages – as it is in a teaching and learning context – it is probably best to allow 'named' contributions only. It might be that learners are allowed to have an 'online identity' but this should be known to the facilitator so postings can be managed appropriately.
- 'Lurkers' – you may come across this term in the literature and it refers to people who access the discussion area and read other contributions but make minimal, if any, posting themselves. This is the equivalent of the silent learner in the classroom. It could be they lack the confidence to contribute or may prefer not to. It is open to debate as to whether that individual is learning and the extent to which they should be persuaded or expected to provide a contribution.

Variations

- Online discussion areas offer the potential for groups who are separated by time or distance to come together to share and discuss ideas. These could include:
  - learners who have successfully completed the course could be invited to join a group of current learners;
  - learners from different year groups on a particular course could come together;
  - learners from different courses could be brought together to explore a topic from a cross-curriculum perspective e.g. Business Studies learners working with Health and Social Care, Art and Design learners working with Performing Arts learners.
- An 'expert in the field' could be invited to join the forum to answer questions or explore a problem with a group of learners. This could be someone with particular knowledge and expertise, an employer, an academic, a careers advisor, a politician, etc.
- Learners could be given a particular role in organizing or managing the discussion forum, e.g. the 'oracle' who is responsible for answering questions, the 'facilitator' who could be responsible for checking participants are contributing and encouraging the 'shy' participants, the 'timekeeper' who can manage the length of time a particular discussion thread is going to run and providing reminders so the group is aware of this.

Subject specialist examples

- *Health and Social Care* – or other specialisms which include a period of work placement.

Learners may feel isolated from their tutors and peers when they attend their work placement, especially if they are away from their regular classroom base for a period of time. A discussion area can be helpful in maintaining contacts with the rest of the group. Learners could be invited to share experiences of specific aspects of their placement experience.

- *Social Sciences* – including History, Politics or Education.

When meeting these subjects for the first time, learners may find it helpful to develop an awareness and personal insight by considering their own attitudes and value position. Such insight might help them to reflect upon this in relation to political events, academic argument or research findings.

A useful tool for this would be to direct learners towards a web-based questionnaire which on completion would provide them with a personal profile of their value position. While it could be said that such tools provide only a crude assessment, nonetheless they can be helpful catalysts for discussion. Given this is a web-based activity, a natural progression would be that learners then go to a designated discussion forum which you will have set up on a secure web environment, typically your institution's Virtual Learning Environment/intranet. Here individual learners could share their reflections of their personal profiles and discuss them in relation to a specific political initiative or contentious statement of your/their choice.

Individual learners can access the Political Compass website to take the test at: http://www.politicalcompass.org/index.

Thinking points

- To what extent do you agree with this statement: 'A learner's learning is limited if their participation in the discussion forum is limited to "lurking".'
- What might be some reasons for the 'lurker's' reluctance to participate?
- How might you encourage the 'lurkers' in your group to participate?
- How would you manage a learner who seems to monopolize the discussion area?

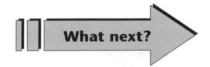

What next?

If you are interested in knowing more about the principles of online learning and ideas for e-learning activities you could try:

Jacques, D. and Salmon, G. (2007) *Learning in Groups: A Handbook for Face-to-face and Online Environments*. London: Routledge.

Salmon, G. (2002) *E-tivities: The Key to Active Online Learning*. London: Kogan Page.

Salmon, G. (2003) *E Moderating: The Key to Teaching and Learning Online*. London: Routledge Falmer.

Stephenson, J. (2001) *Teaching and Learning Online: New Pedagogies for New Technologies (Creating Success)*. London: Kogan Page.

A useful document on online tutoring skills and facilitating online groups can be found at: http://otis.scotcit.ac.uk/casestudy/white.doc.

39 Changing Rooms

 To encourage creativity and learning in the classroom, consider both the layout of the furniture and the amount of stimulating, colourful and visual information around the room and on the walls. Sometimes teachers have little choice over the layout due to fixed furniture, for example, in a science laboratory – but often teachers have scope to rearrange the layout to suit the activities planned. This can have an impact on the interaction between learners and the tutor and the overall success of the activity.

What to do

1   To encourage creativity among learners, try to avoid conventional rows of seats as this is not always conducive to a creative atmosphere. If possible, put desks together for small group collaborative tasks or in a horseshoe configuration for whole-class discussions. If the size of the room does not accommodate these layouts, then perhaps rotate the desks to face a different wall for a change. This may not be practical, however, if there is a fixed whiteboard or projector screen in the room.

2   Learners need to feel comfortable in the room – open windows if it is too hot or, if it is cold, ask them to do a physical activity before starting the lesson, like running on the spot or 'jumping jacks' as a warm-up. This can often help a group to be more active and responsive, especially if they have just come from sitting in another classroom!

3   In sunny rooms, make use of the blinds or, if it tends to be gloomy, consider brightening it with colourful displays including silver foil and mirrors to encourage more light.

4   Although as a teacher you are often limited by the actual physical characteristics of the room, much can be done to improve the surroundings inside. Colourful and lively displays can create a stimulating and interesting learning environment.

5   Music can be used effectively as well. According to Duckett and Tatarkowski (2005), research has shown that alpha or Baroque music is good for learners when they are studying as it has a calming effect and helps them become mentally prepared for work. This is often referred to as the 'Mozart effect'. Alpha music is ideal at the start of a lesson or when concentration is required on a task. Beta or pop music can be effective when learners need to be active.

6   Mobiles hanging from the ceiling, with key words from topics, can produce effective displays. In groups, learners can produce these from card, string, slide binders, coat hangers, and so on and then attach the key words using sticky notes. The key words can have definitions attached to the back of the card or on the mobile or, alternatively, can be referred to by the tutor during teaching. Prizes can be awarded for the most interesting designs. By having the words continually displayed, learners will become more and more familiar with them and the novel way of displaying them will help them remember the terms.

7   Other ways to liven up drab walls and rooms are to produce posters or other artefacts. This

can be a good way to tackle a complex topic. Each group can be given one aspect of the subject to display and then use interesting ways to do this. For example, the display could be a board game, a sculpture, a book or a poem.

8   Encourage the learners to use colour in their displays by using diagrams, pictures, fabrics and photos.

Practical tips

- Posters and displays are often best produced in small groups to encourage active participation by all learners and promote greater creativity. Care needs to be taken to ensure that all learners play an equal part in producing a display.

! Danger points

- It is important that information being gathered is checked for accuracy, as incorrect details could cause confusion and misunderstanding.
- Informative posters may need to be removed if the room is being used for external examinations.
- Care may need to be taken to ensure that there is not too much sensory stimulation in the classroom as this can be counter-productive for some learners with specific learning difficulties and disabilities.

Variations

- Creating mobiles can provide a very good ending for the last part of a lesson. Put the class into groups and, on their mobile they have made, ask them to write the parts of the lesson they have understood on one coloured sticky note and, on another different coloured sticky note, areas of the lesson where they need further help in future. This will help the tutor plan any recapping required during the next lesson.
- Areas of the room can be devoted to key issues or specific revision points. The tutor can divert from the planned lesson to focus on one of these designated areas before returning to the intended plan. This approach can be particularly helpful if interest or concentration is waning during a lesson.
- Designate areas of the classroom for specific activity, for example, a 'quiet' or 'time out area' which might be useful in managing behaviour problems on occasions, or a 'chat area' where small groups can break out from the main lesson to work together.

Subject specialist examples

- *Business* – Posters on the money cycle; explaining sources of finance; elements of a profit and loss account and balance sheet.
- *English* – a timeline for an author/writer with images and text excerpts.
- *Health and Social Care* – infection control posters which could be used as prompts in a care setting as reminders to the staff and members of the public.
- *Performing Arts* – poster for the production of a play.
- *Science* – create and display the solar system in the form of mobiles.
- *Travel and Tourism* – flowchart which shows how to book a holiday.

What next?

Duckett, J. and Tatarkowski, M. (2005) *Practical Strategies for Learning and Teaching on Vocational Programmes*. London: Learning and Skills Development Agency. See page 91 for some information on this book.

40 Character Biography Cards

 Role play activities can promote learning in the affective domain; they can be very useful in challenging stereotypes and developing problem-solving skills. However, lack of learner experience and structure can cause the activity to 'drift' and become ineffective. By using a ready-made character the learner is 'distanced' from a personal view and is encouraged to explore a given scenario from a different perspective.

What to do

1 Prepare a scenario and a character list which is circulated to participating students.
2 Prepare a series of cards for named characters. Provide some details as to values, opinions, remit, age and background of the character to establish a sense of identity.
3 Provide the group with 'rules' regarding timing, conduct and so on.
4 Allow the learners some time to absorb the information on the card and develop the character further.
5 Appoint a chairperson (not representing a character) whose job it is to introduce the scenario, invite opinion and manage the discussion.
6 The learners then assume their character and role play their given scenario under the direction of the chairperson.

Practical tips

- Limit the number of characters; it may be better to have several groups to ensure all learners are engaged.
- Allow sufficient time to review the activity and debrief the learners.
- Try to ensure your selection of characters reflects a diverse mix and includes minority or under-represented groups.

! Danger points

- It may be wise to avoid use of the term 'role play' as it can have negative connotations for some learners. Use alternative language such as 'scenario-based learning'

Variations

- Provide a 'props' box to add an element of fun and help the learner to associate more closely with the character. For example, a selection of hats, a clipboard, spectacles and a walking stick can be sourced quite easily from charity shops.
- Learners could source appropriate artefacts and costumes which substantiate their character.
- A new and unexpected character could be introduced at the discretion of the teacher or chairperson.
- Further challenges to the learner could be provided by spontaneous events occurring as the scenario unfolds.
- Adopt certain characters as a thread throughout a module – they can provide a perspective for all discussions and can help learners to contextualize new knowledge.
- Provide a random selection of appropriate skills, qualities and characteristics. Students on work-based learning programmes can use these to 'profile' job specifications and identify opportunities.

Subject specialist examples

- *Art and Design* – learners can select from a large variety of cards relating to the work of several artists, identifying one and using the information gained to produce a mini autobiography which they present in character to the rest of the group.
- *Construction* – learners construct characters who may have an interest in the work being carried out on a construction site. These could include employees, clients, local residents and architects. Each learner then contributes to a discussion relating to a given scenario.
- *Hair and Beauty* – learners can devise a 'new look' plan for named characters appearing in a television 'soap'.
- *Health and Social Care* – learners can create characters in order to challenge stereotypes of disability. The learners can be encouraged to explore the characteristics and needs of the character, not the disability.
- *Law* – learners discuss a case assuming the characters of a client, solicitor and other people who may be pertinent to the given scenario.

Thinking points

What wider key skills can be developed through engaging with this activity?

41 Wear Your Learning

 This is an alternative way to review learning. Learners are asked to make and 'wear' large sheets of paper on which they document and record key aspects of their learning. Reviews can reinforce and help learners to make sense of and consolidate what they have learned. An additional benefit of reviews which require the active participation of learners can be the opportunity they allow for informal assessment by the teacher.

Encouraging learners to reflect on their learning and experiences can help them to develop further in the future and this activity may also be used as a visual form of reflective practice. Some learners can initially find the writing element of 'reflective practice' difficult when they are asked to convert what may be swirling around in their minds into sentences. Visual representation may be a helpful starting point for such learners.

What to do

1 Provide a plentiful selection of pens, markers, scissors, tape and flip chart paper. Lining paper used for decorating or the reverse side of cheap wallpaper can also be used.
2 Ask learners to make a simple tabard, cape or poncho from the paper.
3 Learners are then asked to review their learning by writing, drawing, printing or stitching their item of paper clothing.
4 Encourage the use of key words, symbolism and pictorial representation.
5 Ask each learner in turn to model their item to the class.

Variations

- Hold a catwalk show or parade with music.
- Take photographs for a permanent record.
- Encourage learners to be reflective and to consider the colour, placing and scale of words, letters and images. The addition of flaps, pockets and holes could be significant and representative. For example, ask learners to use large, bold lettering for subjects they feel confident about and small letters for subjects where they feel they lack knowledge and confidence. A hole could represent a gap or hole in their knowledge. Hidden thoughts, 'grey areas' and uncertainty about a subject could be expressed in pockets and under flaps.
- Encourage learners to think about their learning in different domains, for example, in the affective domain, learners would consider their emotional response to something or their developing attitudes and values.
- Capes or cloaks could be made larger and more theatrical through the use of old, large sheets.
- Head dresses and other accessories could be optional extras.

- Ask learners to bring in an old, large shirt, work overall or t-shirt at the start of a course, module or unit. This could be worked on at the end of a lesson or for homework over a period of time as a form of visual reflective diary. Fabric paints can enhance visual appeal.

Subject specialist examples

- *Anatomy and Physiology* – Use 'Post-it' notes to label a group member, for example, correctly position certain bones or muscles.
- *Art and Design* – A garment worked over the period of a project could record creative dilemmas, decisions, processes, reflective thoughts, difficulties, sources of inspiration, the development of ideas and breakthroughs.
- *Dance* – Learners are given an item of clothing, for example, a shoe and are asked to create a dance based on the item (maybe using it).
- *Drama* – Learners create a character based on an item of clothing.
- *Health and Social Care* – Learners could record their responses to ethical issues and dilemmas. The front and back could portray different viewpoints.

Thinking points

- Some learners may be initially reluctant to participate in what they see as 'dressing up'. How would you encourage their involvement?
- Issues connected to personal expression, disclosure and 'private thoughts made public' will need sensitive handling. What particular strategies might you need to consider in preparing and facilitating such sensitivities?

What next?

Roger Greenaway's website http://reviewing.co.uk is designed for trainers and has a particular focus on outdoor and outward-bound activities. However, it has many ideas for 'reviewing' learning which can easily be adapted to classroom situations.

42 Headaches and Aspirins

This activity can be adapted to use in many different situations. The resources required are cheap and easy to make. It is a useful 'filler' activity if you want something quick to introduce or want to revisit a topic or revitalize your learners! However, it can also be extended to become a more lengthy and substantial activity.

   The idea of the activity is to encourage learners to work together in pairs and offer their own solutions to problems or difficult situations.

What to do

You will need to prepare a set of cards similar to those shown in Figure 42.1. The easiest way to do this is to create sheets of the different cards and then cut them up to the required size. Once you are happy with your design and layout, it is best to laminate the cards to protect them. The learners will be handling the cards and you will hopefully want to use the cards on more than one occasion!

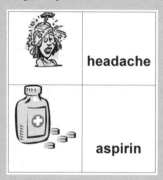

Figure 42.1

1 At the start of the activity, ask each learner to write down a problem they would like an answer to.
2 Hand out the laminated cards so that one half of the group has aspirin cards and the other half each has a headache card. Learners with a headache card are now referred to as the 'headaches' and those with an aspirin card are 'aspirins'.
3 Ask the 'headaches' to stay in their seats and the 'aspirins' to take their card and sit next to a 'headache'. It is important to be quite strict with the rules on timing and talking.

When everyone is paired up, explain the next part of the activity to the learners:

4 The headache tells the aspirin the problem they have written down. The aspirin listens.
5 The aspirins then offer their solutions to the problems. The headaches listen and at this point should not speak or discuss the solutions the aspirins are giving.
6 It is important to limit the time for this part of the activity. Usually 4–5 minutes is best to begin with.
7 When the time is up, the aspirins move on and find a different headache to work with.

8 Repeat the activity, so that the aspirins provide their solutions to a different headache.
9 After three or four rounds, the headaches and aspirins can change round so that the aspirins become headaches and have a chance to collect solutions to their problem.

By the end of the activity, each learner should have several solutions to their original problem. They can then reflect on the ideas and reject or develop them further.

Practical tips

- Timing is essential with this activity – it is better to be 'short and snappy' and allow limited time for each pairing. Move people on while the conversation is still lively, rather than waiting and losing the focus.
- If possible, provide sufficient room so that pairs can have some 'dedicated space' for their exchanges. This can help to minimize distractions and 'eavesdropping'!
- 'Headaches' should be listening rather than engaging in discussion – or rejecting the ideas offered by 'aspirins'.
- Some 'headaches' might want to make notes during the activity of the solutions they are given by their 'aspirin'.
- Build in some time at the end for reviewing and recording information and ideas gathered.

! Danger points

- There may be health and safety issues to consider if learners are moving around the room during this activity.

Variations

- If you are working with a very large group, for example, in a formal lecture, movement around the room might not be practical. A shortened version of the activity could be done whereby learners work with the person on either side of them.

Subject specialist examples

- *Entry to Employment* – to explore anxieties learners may have regarding performance at interviews.
- *Study Skills* – to consider common problems such as time management or assignment work.
- *Vocational Courses* – to explore problems which may have arisen for learners during their work placement.

43 Wikis at Work

 A wiki is a web-based document which individuals can access to add, remove and amend the content. Free wiki software is available on the internet and can be set up relatively easily. Access to a wiki can be public so that anyone can access it or private so that only specific users can join to view and edit the pages.

This activity is useful for engaging large groups of learners online, as it encourages all of them to participate and to discover information for themselves and also it builds up a bank of useful resources which can be shared among all participants. It allows a group of learners to work together, at the same time on one document, such as formulating a joint project or essay, even if they are in different locations.

What to do

1 Learners need access to a computer with the internet and which has the wiki software available. Most educational establishments have these facilities available to their learners or they can be easily downloaded from the internet.

2 The teacher provides a table of questions relating to a topic that is being studied.

3 Each learner has to sign their name against one of the questions offered. It is the responsibility of each learner to research their question and produce appropriate information to create a page on the wiki.

4 Each learner creates some content on their own wiki page which is checked for accuracy by the teacher.

5 Other learners can then view and contribute their own ideas to the various pages on the wiki, building up a series of shared pages edited by the group.

6 Links can be made between different learners' work to produce a bank of information which can be shared. This 'contributing student' approach (Collis and Moonen 2006) encourages them to research and find out information for themselves.

7 Annotated bibliographies can be attached to the work to help learners select and review useful and relevant sources about the subject.

8 Ask learners to compile a 'Frequently Asked Questions' sheet for the topic too. This helps the information gathered to be focused and relevant, and to support others who are unfamiliar with the subject.

9 The teacher should provide an exemplar of good practice for the learners to be aware of the scope and possibilities of their research. For example, the wiki could include video clips, drawings, pictures and music, as well as written information.

Practical tips

- If the course is run online, it may be possible that the learners have no face-to-face contact, and so know little about each other. To help form relationships between the learners, participants could provide a profile of themselves including their interests, hobbies and photos. This will make working together easier and more interactive.
- Most wiki software is set up to send an email alert to all the participants each time changes are made to a wiki.

! Danger points

- For this type of activity, learners need to be familiar with computers and to have regular access to the internet. Some learners may need basic training before they are able to use the software.
- Someone will need to be responsible for checking the work in progress to ensure a user does not attempt to sabotage the wiki! This monitoring may be undertaken by the teacher but the role could also be delegated to a learner.
- Learners need to be advised of any guidelines for appropriate use of the wiki in relation to content, general rules and 'netiquette'.

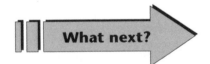

What next?

Wikis can be set up by using software such as:

http://pbwiki.com/.

http://www.wetpaint.com/.

http://www.wikispaces.com/.

When introducing the concept and use of wikis to learners a humorous, annotated clip is available on YouTube which explains wikis in 'Plain English'.

Collis, B. and Moonen, J. (2006) The contributing student: Learners as co-developers of learning resources for reuse in Web environments, in Hung, D. and Khine, M. S. (eds) *Engaged Learning with Emerging Technologies*. Dordrecht: Springer, pp. 49–67.

44 Paper Chains

 In this activity, learners work together to produce a paper chain which links together relevant ideas or facts relating to a particular topic.

The combination of colour and a kinaesthetic activity may enable some learners to 'see' the learning more clearly.

Completed chains could be used to decorate the teaching areas and provide a visual reinforcement and reminder of key learning points. This can be fun with a purpose at certain times of the year when learners like to provide festive decorations.

What to do

1 Prepare a series of cards relating to the subject matter recently taught.
2 Split the learners into two teams and issue each team with a number of pre-gummed paper slips.
3 The tutor selects one of the cards and the teams take it in turns to demonstrate their learning by contributing a word or phrase about that topic.
4 If the answer is approved by the tutor, the learner writes the fact on the slip – sticks the ends together and passes it to the next learner who adds on another word or statement and so on. Each chain is usually worth one point although the tutor can award bonus points for particularly good answers.
5 The chain is completed when neither team has anything more to contribute.
6 The winning team is the one with most points.

Practical tips

- The choice of subject on the card must allow for a good range of contributions to ensure that the chain can reach a reasonable length.
- Paper strips can perhaps be provided by an enterprise project operating within the organization.
- Provide a dampened sponge for moistening the sticky areas.

Variations

- Each learner writes what they know about a new topic on a paper slip. These slips are joined and attached horizontally to the whiteboard at the start of the session. At the end of the session the each learner contributes a piece of new learning which is attached vertically to the existing chain. The tutor uses the 'new' chains as a basis for recap questioning at the start of the next session.

- A chain can be used as an alternative strategy to a thought shower when opening up a topic.
- If space allows, a 'learning tree' can be set up in the classroom and chains hung on the branches for reference.
- Timelines can be produced to provide background knowledge for some subjects.

Subject specialist examples

- *Basic Skills* – learners can be helped to experience the abstract concept of, for example, the number 12 as three blocks of four or two blocks of six, and so on by making number chains.
- *Business Studies* – learners work in two teams and are asked to represent the recruitment and selection process as a horizontal paper chain. Extra pieces of chain can be added to hang vertically, demonstrating underpinning knowledge of each stage of the process. Learners are then asked to explain their representation to the other team.
- *Health and Social Care* – learners can produce a timeline for legislation.
- *Science* – learners can use chains to show the formulae which represent elements, molecules and compounds.
- *SLDD* – learners can have pre-written slips, which may be images or words, which are joined to reinforce the flow of simple tasks.

Thinking points

These paper chains can be displayed to provide a visual reminder and reinforcement of key learning points. How might you or your learners create other interesting and creative visual reminders in the classroom?

45 Cluster Cards

This activity is based on the principle of 'mixing and matching' cards to form groups or 'clusters' of cards which match or belong together. It works well with learners in pairs or groups of three and can be an effective exercise to help to consolidate learning. It is particularly useful for providing visual representation of theoretical concepts and ideas. The activity also has visual appeal as learners are matching text, symbols and pictorial representations and not relying solely on text recognition. The teacher needs to prepare the sets of cards in advance.

What to do

Preparing the cluster cards

1 Select the subject, one which ideally has several 'branches', themes or associated theories. For example, learning theory in 'Psychology' can be broken down into broad headings such as 'Behaviourism', 'Cognitivism' and 'Humanism'.
2 For each of the themes make a list of key words and phrases, associated names and principles.
3 Consider how any of the selected words could be represented pictorially or by a symbol, and select appropriate clip art.
4 Create a 'table' for each theme, for example, using Word. A table of three columns and six rows works well (see Figure 45.1).

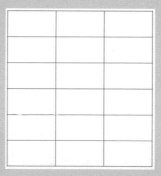

Figure 45.1

5 Into each 'cell' of the table insert a separate word, symbol or image.
6 Complete a table for each theme.
7 Photocopy or print out a set for each pair or group of three to use. Laminate each sheet and cut out each cell from the table.

Using the cluster cards

1 Provide each pair or group with a set of cards.
2 Explain the task is to sort and match the cards into connecting clusters (see Figure 45.2).

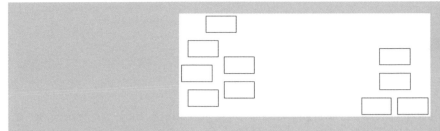

Figure 45.2

3   When learners have completed the task, show the whole tables for them to check against. To do this, the tables could be shown using a digital projector. Alternatively, print or photocopy each table onto a transparency for use with a traditional overhead projector.

Practical tips

- It is helpful to print each set onto different coloured pastel paper, for speedy recognition of a whole set of cards at a glance.
- Print onto card or laminate for extra durability.
- Use a large piece of card or paper as a background on which to place the clusters. Black is particularly effective in providing a visual contrast.

Variations

- Make the task more difficult by including some 'spurious' or 'red herring' cards which need to be rejected.
- Introduce an element of competition: a race against the clock, a scored accuracy competition with points awarded or removed for correct or incorrect placement.
- Introduce it as a research activity – research and reference to notes and use of the internet and textbooks are allowed.
- The cards could be displayed to the whole group on an Interactive Whiteboard. Learners are invited in turn to move individual cards into the connecting clusters.

Subject specialist examples

- *Art and Design* – learners sort images, names and key events into a cluster of cards associated with different art movements Pop Art, Op Art and so on.
- *Business Studies* – learners sort names, images, key words and key texts into different organizational theories.
- *English* – learners sort cards of text into clusters of different literary or linguistic techniques, i.e. a metaphor, a simile, a personification or anthropomorphism.

46 Market Square

 In this activity, learners are allocated a topic for which they can 'purchase' information or signposts to appropriate resource material which will aid successful completion of a task. It necessitates prior preparation by the teacher in compiling the information and resources for 'purchase'. The resources and information provide scaffolding for learners and ensure that they are accessing relevant knowledge at an appropriate level. Information-seeking skills can be developed through structured guidance, a valuable step in developing independent learning.

'Market Square' can be used very successfully by small groups as a revision session, or during a review week providing practice in answering examination questions. It is a useful strategy for helping learners to develop skills in planning the structure of written work. Peer learning is an effective strategy especially when discussion and assessment against a model answer are used. The activity promotes inclusivity by giving the teacher opportunities to differentiate the type and amount of guidance given.

What to do

1   Prepare a series of master and briefing sheets.
2   The master sheets specify relevant examination or assignment questions, either in full or in part, which must be answered.
3   Assemble a briefing sheet to accompany each master which will assist learners in producing a comprehensive answer to the question(s) set. The briefing sheet should contain details of a variety of 'signposts' and reference material, for example, websites, books, articles and so on. It may contain key words, short phrases, quotations, photographs or symbols.
4   Use the 'Tables' facility on your computer to compile this information into discrete sections which can be printed on card and easily separated. Some sections should contain more advanced information and detail than others.
5   Laminate and separate the sections. These card sections provide the items for purchase.
6   Number the reverse side of the cards (the higher the number, the more information offered and the greater the purchase price).
7   It is helpful if each master card and the corresponding information 'chunks' are in the same colour.
8   Clear a space in the room and arrange the furniture to make a 'market square'.
9   Decorate tables with coloured paper to resemble market stalls. A few props such as baskets and aprons can add to the fun. Provide an 'honesty box' on each stall.
10 Display copies of relevant books, articles and other resource materials on one stall.
11 Ensure that there is computer access for each group within the market square and that at least one member of each group has speedy keyboard skills.
12 Arrange the resource cards for each question, number uppermost, on a separate stall, if space allows. Provide a 'price list'. Low number cards with basic information will have a lower token value and so on.

13 Allocate working groups and issue master question sheets.
14 Issue each learner with a small number of tokens (between five and 10 works well) and allow 5 minutes for them to exchange their tokens for the unseen cards.
15 Learners then work in their groups using both the purchased cards and their own knowledge to produce a model answer which can be reproduced and given to other groups.
16 The teacher then facilitates discussion and supplements any missing information and corrects misunderstandings.

Practical tips

- Coloured paperclips make fun tokens.
- Consider how the room can be arranged and dismantled without encroaching on learning time.
- Depending on the time available, the level of work and group size, learners may work on one or more tasks.

! Danger points

- Adequate discussion and feedback time is essential so work out and publicize timings at several points in the session.
- Be vigilant to ensure that learners leave their tokens in the 'honesty box' and do not turn over the cards before purchase. If there are Learning Support Staff within the session, perhaps they will assume the role of stall holders, while the teacher acts as Market Superintendent!

Variations

- The briefing sheet can comprise a model answer written in an academic style and separated into paragraphs. Learners are then encouraged to assemble the paragraphs in the correct order and check their work against the original briefing sheet.
- Identify a relevant topic that learners have recently studied. Issue learners with a number of small blank cards and allow a short time for them to write series of key points reflecting their knowledge on the topic; one point for each card. Pose an appropriate assignment or examination question and allow learners a short time to produce a skeleton answer. Each learner can 'swap' cards' (unseen) with any member in the group to help in their task. The teacher then facilitates a discussion allowing learners to develop their answer and to check understanding.
- Have a 'swap shop' for useful resources and websites where learners can trade results of research.

- Set up subject specialist market stalls. Ask learners, working in groups to provide information on a topic for a future session. For example, in a Health and Social Care group studying services for the elderly, each group of learners could provide detailed information on particular services which could be 'purchased' by other groups.

Thinking points

Peer learning and assessment against a model answer can provide valuable reinforcement for learners who struggle to present academic work. In what other ways could you incorporate peer learning and assessment into your teaching?

Review is an essential element of revision and helps to transfer knowledge to the long-term memory. How could you build in opportunities for review at regular intervals?

Alistair Smith's Accelerated Learning Cycle describes four stages: connection, activation, demonstration and consolidation. Do you follow this cycle with your learners?

What next?

Alastair Smith's Accelerated Learning Cycle can be found at http://www.alite.co.uk.

47 Learning Mats

Successful advertising or educational campaigns often rely upon providing people with frequent reminders of key words, phrases or images. These campaigns might appear on television screens, magazines, newspapers and large billboards. The principles which underpin this type of subliminal advertising can be applied to teaching and learning; some of the important learning points which are pertinent to a particular lesson can be incorporated into Learning Mats which are then made available to the learners during the session.

What to do

1   Prepare an A4 sheet with a decorative border of 3–5cm from all edges.
2   Randomly insert words or pictures associated with the session subject into this border, using different fonts and colours (See Figure 47.1).

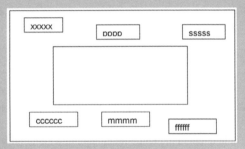

Figure 47.1

3   Photocopy a supply of paper using the template.
4   Have sheets available for learners to make notes during a session, prepare answers to questions and so on.

Practical tips

- Include key words or new vocabulary in the border of the mat to aid memory and to reinforce correct spelling.
- A3 sheets can be provided for group work in a similar way to a mind map.

Variations

- Provide homework tasks or assignment questions on a sheet which incorporates a border containing key vocabulary, submission dates and so on.
- Laminate some mats for use as mini whiteboards in class activities.
- Mouse mats displaying subject-specific vocabulary or generic introductory sentence beginnings can be produced for use in learning centres.
- Produce an assignment scaffold on a learning mat to help less able learners structure their work.
- Learners can design a mind map to record their learning, using the border content as a prompt.
- Ask learners to reflect on aspects of a topic they found difficult and use their computer skills to prepare a learning mat for future groups.
- Learning mats may be transformed into 'doodle mats'. Some people naturally doodle while learning, helping with concentration and expression of thought. The mat offers a relevant place for doodles to be captured!

Subject specialist examples

- *Built Environment* – learners can be provided with a Learning Mat which contains formulae for electrical inputs.
- *English* – if learners have difficulty with the correct use of apostrophes, incorporate some examples into the Learning Mat. You could include, for example, plural nouns, singular and plural possession and contractions.
- *Entry to Employment* – learners can undertake job search activities on a mat which outlines key phrases, words and sentence beginnings.
- *Holistic Therapists* – learners can be given a mat which contains reminders about the essential oils and contraindications.
- *Science* – provide mats for use in laboratory work which include reminders for the learners about health and safety considerations.

Thinking points

Consider a lesson you have recently taught. Now deconstruct it to identify the specific learning points which learners needed to grasp but had some difficulty with during the lesson. How could those learning points be incorporated into a Learning Mat?

48 Learning Museums

 A Learning Museum provides an excellent summative activity allowing learners to reflect on their learning. Learners have the opportunity to produce and select a range of artefacts, such as poems, pictures or objects, representing a topic or experience from the past and to display and annotate them for others to see.

What to do

1 Once a topic has been completed within the module, the learners need to be arranged into groups of three or four.

2 Ask each group to compile or make a display of a selection of artefacts which summarise their learning of the topic. In a museum exhibition, artefacts can take many different forms, including letters, photos, or objects of interest around a topic, such as World War I or History and Development of Sport. Learners could prepare a poem, a web page, a sculpture, a podcast or a collage. This approach encourages the learners to represent their chosen topic in an unusual, creative way.

3 Each learner must contribute at least one artefact to the group's display.

4 Allow the group time to discuss their ideas and to prepare an action plan for their display. Each member of the group needs to produce a different artefact so that different aspects of the topic are represented. The organization and collection of materials and resources might require extra time, so the actual completion of the display might take a couple of lessons.

5 Provide the groups with some basic materials, such as coloured paper, pens and glue to help them plan and design their displays.

6 Allow time for completion of the artefacts. This may take more than one lesson, especially if research and extra resources are required.

7 Once the learners have selected or produced their exhibits, ask them to display them around the room with appropriate explanatory labels attached; especially if the artefact needs further clarification, such as a sculpture or a drawing.

8 Each group explains the symbolism and meaning of their display to the other learners. This will reinforce and check their learning about the topic, by allowing themselves to express creatively how their artefact represents the subject studied. It will also provide a recap of the topic for others in the class.

9 Provide a 'comments book' for the learners to give feedback on each other's displays, and highlight the ones which have provided the most impact on their learning. This could be linked to the assessment of the topic.

10 Give learners time to reflect individually or in their groups on being a participant in the museum exhibition. Ask them to comment on how this had increased their learning while visiting and viewing the other artefacts. Which one had caught their eye? What was it like taking part in such an exercise and what advice could they give to improve it in the future?

Practical tips

- Check the accuracy of the displays if they are going to stay in place for a period of time, otherwise learners could be confused and misled by incorrect information.
- Take the group to visit a museum or encourage the learners to visit one in their spare time. This will help them to visualise how displays are put together and the type of artefacts which are exhibited. If this is not possible, take digital photos of a museum's displays yourself and show them to the group at the start of the activity to help them with their planning.

! Danger points

- Consider how the exhibits can be displayed for long periods without being spoilt or without disrupting the space available for other classes using the room.
- This activity may need to continue into another session before it is completed. Consider how the work in progress can safely be stored until the following lesson.

Variations

- Invite other guests to visit the museum and ask the learners to be museum guides to explain the exhibits to them. These could be learners studying the topic in a different group and therefore helping to embed their knowledge of the topic.
- Open up the room over a lunchtime and ask the group to organise a rota of themselves as curators to look after and explain the exhibits and to collect feedback in the 'comments book'.
- The group could prepare a poster advertising their exhibition. What would be in the 'museum shop' as 'highlights' of this activity that learners could 'take away' as evidence of their learning 'trip'?
- Key artefacts from the displays could be selected by the group and then form a 'museum on loan'. This could be shown to other groups of learners who might be in the year below, as evidence of what to expect from this part of the curriculum. This 'travelling exhibition' could also be used as part of Open Days where groups could introduce their displays to parents, or new learners about to embark on the course or module.
- Learners could use this activity to reflect on their own experiences and achievements on the course or module by producing an individual creative artefact. These displays could be used to motivate or support learners moving up into the next academic year of the course.

49 Ask the Expert

 In this activity, experts are required to pass on knowledge to other learners. Explaining to others helps the 'explainer' to reflect on and organise their own knowledge. The 'learner' can benefit from having information introduced in an easily accessible format. Learners may question more freely within the context of a 'game' and thus gain insight into areas of personal doubt or confusion without consulting the teacher.

What to do

1   Prepare for the activity in advance by inviting questions on recently studied topics.
2   Learners write their questions on a slip of card. It is helpful if each learner contributes at least two cards, one question on each. The teacher also contributes questions.
3   The teacher checks that the learner questions are appropriate and retains them. (It can be fun to keep them in a sparkly top hat!)
4   All appropriate questions are recorded and passed to the experts who can research their answers to possible questions in advance of the session.
5   On the day of the activity rearrange the classroom to provide a 'top table' where a panel of three or four 'experts' selected from the class are seated. Provide notepads and glasses of water to add to the atmosphere.
6   The teacher acts as chairperson and selects random questions from the hat, directing each question to one expert. Other experts can be asked by the chairperson to contribute if there are further points to be drawn out.
7   Some learners may wish to make notes and so a sheet containing all the questions submitted can be provided.

Practical tips

- Allow time for the class to feed back so that any misconceptions and problems can be dealt with
- Summarize the main points, making reference to the information pack.

! Danger points

- Questions contributed by learners may involve lower order thinking skills. The teacher must ensure that their contributions focus on questions involving, for example, synthesis and evaluation.

Variations

- Present the learners with a scenario, for example, a customer receives poor service in a retail outlet. The scenario could be paper-based, describing the experiences of the customer, or a film or DVD excerpt. Learners work in pairs to decide what mistakes have been made and what generally represents good or bad practice in that area. The teacher closes the activity with a discussion confirming and supplementing learner views.
- Learners are provided with a topic title and a range of learning resources. Time is allocated for self-study. Working alone or in groups, the learners prepare a series of questions to test the teacher's knowledge. The teacher sits in the 'hot seat' and fields the questions.
- The class is divided into two teams. The teacher acts as scorekeeper. Learners are issued with a handout or a series of pictures which contain factual or data inaccuracies. (Ensure that these errors represent common subject misconceptions and are not, for example, simple typographical errors.) In their teams, the learners work through the packs identifying and correcting the mistakes. The winning team is the one which identifies and corrects the most errors.
- The teacher selects a topic which the 'teacher' must 'teach' to the learners.
- In a timed period, the 'teacher' reads the information pack and prepares to teach it. At the same time the 'learner' reads the information and prepares a series of questions for the 'teacher'.
- The 'teacher' then teaches and the learner asks questions.

Thinking points

- Do your questioning skills need honing? Are they simply testing recall?
- Could learners in your groups act out scenarios which could be filmed (subject to necessary permissions) for later use?

50 Inside Outside

 A change in routine can enliven learning and surprises can awaken interest and increase motivation. Field trips and external visits may be too expensive for all learners to attend; the teacher may have concerns about organizing and planning travel arrangements. However, your own learning site and immediate locale could well provide a stimulus. Arranging a business class in the college boardroom takes the learning 'outside'. A First Aid lesson can be held in a built environment workshop. Running a mini 'sports day' in a local park can provide a practical element to the topic of Event Planning. The bus station can encourage a piece of creative writing or the development of numeracy skills in planning a series of journeys using the information sources available.

Alternatively, the classroom could be transformed to bring the outdoors indoors and provide multi-sensory immersion to stimulate learning. This is only practical when a classroom does not have to be returned to its normal state within a short time scale. Setting up a seashore, with sand, shells, pieces of fishing netting, providing appropriate sound effects, for example, waves crashing, seagulls calling, can provide a cross-curriculum focus for various groups 'visiting the seaside'.

Practical tips

- Risk analysis must be completed and appropriate organizational procedures followed.
- Learners need to be well prepared if they are to gain maximum learning from the experience. Provide a list of questions to be answered on return to base, prepare a 'what to look out for' sheet, and so on. Adequate debriefing following a visit is essential.
- Take photographs of learners involved in tasks, use these as a corridor display and run a caption competition with a small prize.

! Danger points

- Some learners may consider a change in routine an excuse for immature behaviour so ensure they are kept busy with clear tasks and deadlines.
- Rules and protocols for behaviour when offsite need to be very clearly communicated.

Subject specialist examples

- *Art and Design* – many art galleries and museums have Education Officers. Liaise with them before planning a visit.
- *Built Environment* – learners could be given a project brief and then visit a builders'

merchants to identify the tools and the materials needed. Core skills development could be facilitated by the costing out of the brief.

- *Early Years* – following an input on play, two learners could visit a local child care setting for a short period and present a report to the remainder of the group on their return.
- *English* – a walk in the countryside could stimulate a discussion on the poetry of Keats or Houseman.
- *Hair and Beauty* – learners could visit a wholesale supplier as part of a business finance module.
- *Health and Social Care* – a 'residents' lounge' could be prepared in a classroom in which some learners could be designated as carers and some as clients.
- *Science* – learners could study water life in the local pond or canal, collecting samples and analysing the ecosystems back in the laboratory.

Thinking points

Consider the classroom to be 'inside' and decide what 'outside' opportunities there are within your organization.

What learning opportunities does the local market afford for your subject?

PART II
Theoretical Framework

Creativity

It is worth observing from the outset that if there were ever a concept that belied consensus, creativity would be right up there at the top of the list. Though the emphasis of this book is targeted on practical classroom skills and techniques to further the facilitative approach, rather than the didactic, it is worth dwelling upon some elements of the creativity debate in an effort to contextualize such practice within a theoretical framework.

'Creativity' has been debated and discussed in several areas of education for many years now: Early Years, Primary teaching; Art and Design Education (Lytton 1971; Slater 1971; Duffy 1998; Craft 2000). It has become a buzz word in the UK in policy debates, yet recently articles and letters in the educational press have focused on how the current climate of testing across the education system may be constraining teachers' 'creativity'.

The activities provided in this book will hopefully allow teachers to further enhance their creative and innovative approaches to their teaching and learning set within debates surrounding research and theoretical knowledge.

Creativity is an elusive, slippery creature. Perhaps a logical starting point would be the acceptance of a definition from which creative practice would be operationalized. The difficulty facing practitioners who wish to engage in creative teaching is that without consensus there is no identifiable definition that commands sufficient support to achieve this. All practitioners can be aware of is the debate that surrounds the concept and a positioning of one's efforts on the map of the terrain, however, even this is shifting sand. It might be observed that for practitioners to identify their creative practices, a good deal of energy would need to be expended in staking out the particular qualification of the term that bestows meaning on classroom activity.

This is no small matter. Like many other key terms in educational pedagogy, creativity is a volatile and powerful concept that illuminates more about practitioner beliefs, meanings and assumptions than any bona fide definition of what creativity is.

We can identify the unfolding of creativity as a map from Plato's view that society needs creative people (Cropley 2001), through the contemporary association of creativity as student-centred learning in the 1970s that prompted UK Prime Minister James Callaghan's view that the pendulum had swung too far by 1976. The 1980s saw creativity refashioned to meet the demands of neo-liberal values associated with innovation and entrepreneurship. There is a sense that it is within this discourse that creativity currently languishes and it will be a feature of this chapter to highlight this part of the map in comparison with other domains that are less well travelled in the current educational milieu.

The current milieu sites creativity in definitions associated with the NACCE research (1999) and the following is indicative of this perspective:

> First [the characteristics of creativity] always involve thinking or behaving imaginatively. Second, overall this imaginative activity is purposeful: that is, it is directed to achieving an objective. Third, these processes must generate something original. Fourth, the outcome must be of value in relation to the objective. (NACCE 1999: 4)

On first reading, this appears to offer practitioners a clear guide to their practice. Classroom activities can be mapped against such a four-point plan and if the answer is yes on the four counts identified in the definition, then creativity can be said to be occurring. This can be extended both to elements of teaching – 'Am I being a creative practitioner?' – as well as to a consideration of how it is that learners are learning.

When examined more closely, however, the difficulties with such a definition begin to emerge. To say that thinking or behaving imaginatively qualifies creativity is to locate the concept in a psychological process, that is, for creativity to be occurring, it must be the product of the mental processes of an individual. In this definition, creativity becomes, like intelligence, an essence to be identified, quantified and measured. Though meeting the requirements and demands of neo-liberal practices, there is unease among educationalists at such a positioning of creativity. Bleakley is one who asks the question:

> The issue raised here is why certain constructions of creativity become legitimised at a certain point in history to the detriment of other possibilities. This has clear implications for teaching in higher education where 'creativity' is seen as a desirable learning outcome, for we must ask what kind of creativity is judged as desirable and what is excluded as illegitimate? . . . What for example are the legitimating mechanisms that have led to studies of creativity becoming dominated by the discipline of psychology? (Bleakley 2004: 465)

The first critique of the definition then suggests that to attribute creativity to individualized thinking or imagination shows a predominant reductionism approach that places huge constraints on what creativity might possibly be.

The second and third parts of the definition offer further contradictions. We are told that there must be a purposeful outcome resulting from the exercise of imaginative thinking and that this must be something original. Is there not something of a contradiction in terms here? Allowing that creativity is reduced to the product of individual thought and imagination, how would we know that something original was purposeful? On this basis, most art would not manifest as creative – it has no *purpose* though it might be original (Bleakley 2004). The requirement that creativity be purposeful merely identifies the valorization of the concept in utilitarian terms, something that we might expect of the instrumentality inherent in neo-liberal thought and practice. It also places creativity in a framework whereby a community of practitioners or experts place value on the ideas and products of those in a domain of practice. The recognition of this process already signifies that creativity is being identified as far more than the culmination of an individual's thinking capacities. What is lost from the definition is that it excludes those who do not create within the parameters of the community of practice which dictates what is to be positively sanctioned. An observation from research on a trainee tutor in Further Education illuminates the point:

> I'd say I had three students who were creative. Ironically, they'll never make it in the industry – they're loose cannons, they don't conform to accepted practices and their lifestyles bar them from inclusion in productive projects. But they're way beyond the others when it comes to creativity. (Ormondroyd and Eastwood 2007)

The sentiment is captured by Kael, 'In this country we encourage creativity among the mediocre but real bursting creativity appals us. We put it down as undisciplined, as somehow "too much"' (cited in Maggio 1994: 42).

We consider that it has been worth dwelling on the orthodox definition of creativity in order to see that the section of the map that it illuminates draws heavily on the notions of individual thinking processes, psychological conceptualizations of creativity and an inherent utilitarian orientation. These are extended to include both creativity as teaching and creativity as learning. The consequences of this view will be discussed later, but what of alternative definitions for the practitioner, given the limitations of the orthodox perspective?

As long ago as 1945, Fritz bemoaned the location of education practitioners as engaging in a 'reactive response orientation' rather than an 'orientation of the creative', as cited in Craft (1997: 85–6). From the viewpoint of the creative practitioner, one might argue that contemporary practitioners are far more constrained than has previously been the case. The operation within a field of international, national and local organizational constraint defines structures and shapes not only curriculum issues, but the actual identities of learners and tutors all the way through the educational system. The recognition of such constraints poses a challenge to creative teaching, however it is defined. The teaching profession, while demanding creativity does not, in fact, foster it in its members (Woods 1995: 84).

Craft suggests there are several barriers to professional creativity:

> The complexity of the role of the teacher and the breadth of the job are the two common reasons for resistance. Others include the general overload of the job, change fatigue and cynicism stemming from perceptions of an experience of external judgements/inducements such as Ofsted inspections ... If creativity is perceived, erroneously as a new curriculum subject rather than an aspect of all subjects which enables mastery, then curriculum overload is another reason cited for not wanting to develop with this in mind. (2000: 135)

Avis et al. (2001: 75–6) also demonstrate that the world of Further Education shows 'the intensification of labour. Lecturers consistently worked over hours, where we gained a sense of an over-burdened profession.'

Since that research, the neo-liberal practices first implanted in Further Education have increasingly become familiar to practitioners in schools and Higher Education too. The implementation of managerial regimes throughout organizations in the United Kingdom has been a feature of the success of the system's ability to colonize what once were public sector domains of practice.

Such regimes operate with a zeal that is associated with 'faith' by Clarke and Newman (1997). The impact of regulatory audit mechanisms on practitioners is well documented and requires no further assertion here, but its impact upon the creative risk-taking elements of a practitioner is observable. Given over three decades of such practice, practitioners are constructed by a discourse that demands obedience, conformity, loyalty to cultural practices that laud technical proficiency and efficiency and results in a product-orientated curriculum over imaginative, exploratory and deep learning techniques. One might ask in such an infertile environment, where is the support to be found for creative teaching?

In order that creative teaching and learning be facilitated, there is a requirement that practitioners have the ability to operate outside and beyond the parameters set as acceptable and valuable by the very organizational fabric itself. To be creative is to have a perception of possibility, to see potentially new options. These are elusive for both learners and practitioners within the current system of constraining discourses.

Bleakley (2004) allows some mapping of creativity that provides a fruitful alternative for the creative practitioner. His emphasis on social construction allows practitioners to see that creativity always sits at the nexus of tutors, learners and the historical meanings and valorization of creativity. Creativity is not a fixed essence, but rather a discourse that operates as a moving feast, carving out domains of meaning and practice that sometimes are positively valued while at other times are negatively sanctioned. Of Bleakley's 10 discourses on creativity, it could be argued that only two are highly valued by the current system – creativity as ordering, creativity as problem solving. This leaves eight discourses that are either ignored or negatively sanctioned.

Bleakley (2004) allows the practitioner to qualify creativity and locate it on the larger map. One also becomes aware of 'possibility' by familiarizing oneself with the other eight discourses. We might also recognise that this typology is not exhaustive, but it does provide a contextual framework for qualifying what we mean by creativity.

A pithier critique of creativity in education is provided by Howard Gibson (2005), who argues that on two counts, that of its association with instrumental reason and that of its reification by Romantic thought, creativity is done a great disservice. On the one hand, the orthodox definition previously discussed merely makes creativity a handmaid to the demands of narrow economic values. It neglects the contextualization of such values, 'Like Fagin, teaching Oliver innovative and creative methods for thieving that would increase the production of stolen handkerchiefs the substantive value of stealing per se remains unquestioned' (Gibson 2005: 156).

Both Craft (2001) and Gibson (2005) see the necessity of debate about the way that creativity depends upon cultural norms and meanings. Gibson is adamant that a vocabulary needs to be implemented to distinguish alternative interpretations of what creativity might possibly be, contrasted to the concept of 'createndentious', which defines the current fashion of binding creativity firmly to narrow economic values.

He is also concerned about the over-psychologized aspects of creativity and the foundation of such assumptions in the Romantic tradition. For Gibson, free expression is a conceptual misnomer. The idea of individual creativity is similarly flawed in that it presupposes a subjectivity which is over-simplistic and devoid of the cultural milieu which both shapes and moulds it.

The idea that learners should develop their own creative talents (Blair 2001) is an example of this mode of thought and it is deeply reinforced in neo-liberal rhetoric. The plain observation that people have neither choices nor the skills to make them is excluded from such thought. We are decision-making creatures and we make decisions informed by past experience and future aspiration. Choices are of a very different order of action and incorporate aspects of creativity that lie well outside its current confinement in orthodox definitions.

Gibson's (2005) work soundly interrogates the concept of creativity in allowing us to see what it is not. When confined to the domain of instrumental reason or to the supposed indwelling capacity for creative thinking, creativity is robbed of its potential and capacity to liberate and transcend. Indeed, within such confines, creativity becomes identified with certainty, whereas Fromm (1997) argues that, 'Creativity requires the courage to let go of certainties.' It is this last domain, the location of creativity in its philosophical context, that education has ignored – yet within this domain creativity is at its most powerful.

Ontological developments in the language and meanings deriving from the natural sciences show creativity at its most potent in terms of re-fashioning perceptions of reality. Education seems reluctant to engage with breakthroughs in this domain. This is probably a consequence of an orthodox hegemony that seeks to ground human experience in a purely economic and business model of reality.

However, it can be seen that in this domain, creativity as consciousness is hugely significant. For Whitehead (1990), it represented the universal, that which pre-empted reality. Bohm's (1998) theorizing of the 'implicate' and 'explicate' order, drew attention to the redundancy of making distinctions between subject and object as does Pirsig's (1992) work on the metaphysics of quality. In Goswami's (1995) work, consciousness precedes matter; creativity becomes the universe's architect. Yet, education maintains the traditional view of the learner as though individuals are exactly that, bracketed off from the social, natural and cosmic environment. If creativity is engaging with new perceptions, education might well benefit from at least investigating the ones that lie currently outside its purview; though in the current climate this is hardly likely. To see creativity as a relational nexus of being de-emphasizes the whole concept of the individual and thinking becomes a redundant concept. A bridge far too far for current educational practice, but creative nevertheless.

In conclusion, the engagement with creativity by practitioners in education is fraught with challenge.

The use of the term is restricted, as Gibson (2005) demonstrates. Confined within a framework to boundaries set up by business models of practice and psychological assumptions about thinking, creativity rarely breaks out to fulfil its potential. On the plus side, practitioners might be applauded for examining and expanding techniques of learning. The recognition that learners learn more by active engagement with knowledge and skills, rather than passive receivership has been a feature of the contribution made by 'small creativity' to educational practice. This book offers a range of such practical activities. All are designed to involve students actively in their learning. They can be used irrespective of 'subject specialism'. In providing such a range of technical skills, we ask that tutors be mindful of Gibson's Oliver Twist analogy. We have no wish to encourage the how of teacher/learning without a consideration of the wider implications of educational pedagogy. In this, we encourage practitioners to engage with the debate on creativity and to recognise its potential for teaching and learning beyond the narrow confines of the system's current constraints.

Bibliography

Avis, J., Bathmaker, A. and Parsons, J. (2001) Reflections from a time log diary: Towards an analysis of the labour process within further education, *Journal of Vocational and Educational Training*, 53(1): 61–79.

Blair, T. (2001) Foreword by the Prime Minister in *Culture & Creativity: The Next Ten Years*. London: Department for Culture, Media & Sport.

Bleakley, A. (2004) Your creativity or mine? A typology of creativities in higher education and the value of a pluralistic approach, *Teaching in Higher Education*, 9(4): 463–75.

Bohm, D. (1998) *On Creativity*. London: Routledge.

Bradbury, R. (1989) in W. Safire and L. Safire (eds) *Words of Wisdom*. New York: Fireside.

Clarke, J. and Newman, J. (1997) *The Managerial State*. London: Sage.

Craft, A. (2000) *Creativity Across the Primary Curriculum*. London: Routledge.

Craft, A. (2001) *An Analysis of Research and Literature on Creativity in Education*, Report prepared for the Qualifications and Curriculum Authority, London: QCA.

Creativity Centre Ltd (2006) *Facilitating Creativity in Higher Education: The Views of National Teaching Fellows*. Paignton: Creativity Centre Ltd.

Cropley, A. (2001) *Creativity in Education and Learning*. London: Kogan Page.

Duffy, B. (1998) *Supporting Creativity and Imagination in the Early Years*. Buckingham: Open University Press.

Eastwood, L. and Ormondroyd, C. (2007) Creativity: a cautionary tale, unpublished report.

Fromm, E. (1997) The ultimate success, in Quotations Library, available at: www.google.co.uk, accessed 7 June 2008.

Gibson, H. (2005) What creativity isn't: The presumptions of instrumental and individual justification for creativity in education, *British Journal of Education Studies*, 53(2): 148–67.

Goswami, A. (1995) *The Self-Aware Universe*. New York: Tarcher.

Jeffrey, B. and Craft, A. (2001) The universalisation of creativity, in A. Craft., B. Jeffrey and M. Leibling (eds) *Creativity and Education*. London: Continuum.

Lytton, H. (1971) *Creativity and Education*. London: Routledge.

Maggio, R. (ed.) (1994) *The Beacon Book of Quotations by Women*, Boston, MA: Beacon Press.

National Advisory Committee on Creative and Cultural Education (1999) *All Our Future: Creativity, Culture and Education*. London: DFEE Publications.

Pirsig, R. (1992) *Lila: An Enquiry into Morals*. London: Black Swan.

Slater, G. (ed.) (1971) *Education and Creative Work*. Hull: Hull Printers Ltd.

Wragg, T. (2003) in *The Guardian Education*, 10 June.

Index